THE BOARD AND SUPERINTENDENT HANDBOOK

THE BOARD AND SUPERINTENDENT HANDBOOK

Current Issues and Resources

Edited by Amy E. Van Deuren,
Thomas F. Evert, and
Bette A. Lang

Published in partnership with the
American Association of School Administrators

ROWMAN & LITTLEFIELD
Lanham • Boulder • New York • Toronto • London

Published in partnership with the
American Association of School Administrators

Published by Rowman & Littlefield Education
A division of Rowman & Littlefield
4501 Forbes Boulevard, Suite 200, Lanham, Maryland 20706
www.rowman.com

Unit A, Whitacre Mews, 26-34 Stannary Street, London SE11 4AB

Copyright © 2015 by Van Deuren, Evert, and Lang

All rights reserved. No part of this book may be reproduced in any form or by any electronic or mechanical means, including information storage and retrieval systems, without written permission from the publisher, except by a reviewer who may quote passages in a review.

British Library Cataloguing in Publication Information Available

Library of Congress Cataloging-in-Publication Data

The board and superintendent handbook : current issues and resources / edited by Amy E. Van Deuren, Thomas F. Evert, and Bette A. Lang.
    pages cm
  Includes bibliographical references.
  ISBN 978-1-4758-1549-8 (hardback) — ISBN 978-1-4758-1550-4 (pbk.) — ISBN 978-1-4758-1551-1 (e-book) 1. School boards—United States. 2. School board members—United States. 3. School superintendents—United States. 4. School board-superintendent relationships—United States. I. Van Deuren, Amy, 1965– II. Evert, Thomas F., 1947–
  LB2831.B56 2015
  379.1'531—dc23
                                        2015022410

∞™ The paper used in this publication meets the minimum requirements of American National Standard for Information Sciences—Permanence of Paper for Printed Library Materials, ANSI/NISO Z39.48-1992.

Printed in the United States of America

CONTENTS

Acknowledgments   vii

Preface   ix
   Amy E. Van Deuren, Thomas F. Evert, Bette A. Lang

PART I: BOARD/SUPERINTENDENT INTERACTIONS

1   Issues, Contexts, and Frameworks   3
   Amy E. Van Deuren and Thomas F. Evert

PART II: BOARDS AND SUPERINTENDENTS ADDRESS CURRENT ISSUES TOGETHER

2   Understanding the Comprehensive Curriculum Process   13
   Linda Nortier

3   Comprehensive Student Support Systems as Exemplified by RTI: A District Report for Boards and Superintendents   31
   Denise L. Wellnitz and Thomas F. Evert

4   Alternative Compensation Models   47
   Daniel W. Olson and Amy E. Van Deuren

5 What Boards and Superintendents Should Know about the
Importance of Teachers 65
Raymond J. Golarz

6 Technology in Schools: The Role of Boards and Superintendents 71
Valerie Schmitz, Amy E. Van Deuren, and Thomas F. Evert

PART III: RESOURCES

7 Administrative Assistants: A Critical Resource 91
Bette A. Lang and Thomas F. Evert

8 Using External Experts for District Improvement 103
Thomas F. Evert and Amy E. Van Deuren

9 State and National Associations, External Experts,
Search Firms, and Universities 111
Thomas F. Evert and Bette A. Lang

10 Resources, Books, Articles, Dissertations, and Summary
of Selected Research 121

About the Contributors 139

ACKNOWLEDGMENTS

We are indebted to the many students, parents, staff, community members, board members, and superintendents with whom we have associated during our journey in education. Thank you for teaching us so much and for your relentless resolve to make our schools better.

We extend appreciation to the school board members who willingly shared their opinions and insights for this book that we hope will become a useful resource to school leaders. Board members receive much criticism, little praise or remuneration, and keep showing up to fight the good fight for our students. Thank you!

We also thank the many current and retired superintendents who have provided us with valuable information and sage wisdom over the years. Superintendents have demanding, challenging, and rewarding jobs and strive to lead and manage while keeping a laser-like focus on student success.

We also say thank you to a group of unsung heroes in the world of PK–12 public education—administrative assistants. These individuals are deeply committed to the schools and districts they serve. Benjamin Franklin stated, "Energy and persistence conquer all things." These words could be the motto of the talented and dedicated administrative assistants who support both people and processes in their daily work.

Thank you also to the special individuals who served as readers/reviewers and critiqued our book. Board president Jan Berg and superintendent Randy Refsland took time from their extraordinarily busy schedules to share insights and make this book more practitioner-friendly.

We extend a special statement of appreciation to the authors of the chapters in this book. The writers, current and retired practitioners in school administration, have firsthand knowledge of both practical and academic considerations, which added richness, relevance, and depth to this book.

Next, we thank our friends and families for their support. This effort has been a significant undertaking and created periods of highs and lows. Those closest to us kept us pushing forward during difficult junctures. Onward.

Finally, we extend a special thank-you to our trusted friend and colleague, Tom's former administrative assistant to the superintendent, School District of Janesville, Diane Wesner, for her efforts, patience, and skills. Thank you, Diane!

Amy E. Van Deuren
Thomas F. Evert
Bette A. Lang

PREFACE

Amy E. Van Deuren, Thomas F. Evert, Bette A. Lang

The political landscape of America's public schools has undergone major changes in recent years. For example, Wisconsin PK–12 public schools changed when Governor Scott Walker signed into law 2011 Wisconsin Act 10 (Act 10), which strictly limited collective bargaining for most public workers, including teachers and administrators.

Act 10 created new economic and political questions for boards and superintendents regarding district employee contracts. The unions, specifically teacher unions, were placed under the microscope and received much scrutiny. In February 2011, parents, teachers, business leaders, community leaders, and other citizens were caught up in massive rallies at Wisconsin's state capitol for over two weeks, advocating for and against Act 10.

During this time, several game-changing educational concepts and initiatives were gaining popularity throughout the country. Public schools were moving into what Smith, Chavez, and Seaman (2012) describe as the Conceptual Age of education. The Conceptual Age is the next evolutionary stage following the Agricultural, Industrial, and Information ages. It places more emphasis on personalized learning, integration of technology, and results-oriented education.

Strong movements were underway to develop and implement a Common Core curriculum based on specific state standards and assessments. This movement was and is national in focus and has resulted in ongoing political tension in many states. Wisconsin was one of forty-six states to accept the use of the Common Core State Standards, and the Wisconsin Department of Public Instruction (DPI) developed the schedule for implementation in 2010.

Another process being addressed was how to best hold teachers accountable through coaching and evaluation. These state initiatives were being implemented throughout the country. Wisconsin and DPI rolled out teacher supervision in an initiative entitled Educator Effectiveness, which was piloted in the 2013–2014 academic year. Full implementation was slated for the 2014–2015 school year.

Finally, the last several years have seen an in-depth review of and revision of support services for all students, especially at-risk and special education students. The new emphases to reach these students are being implemented in initiatives such as Response to Intervention (RTI) and Positive Behavior Intervention Systems (PBIS). They are designed to ensure a wide variety of scientifically based interventions and techniques in order to identify and provide extra support for struggling students at all levels.

Taken in their totality, Act 10, a new age of learning and use of technology, Common Core State Standards, coaching and evaluation, and changes in student support services, exponential demands are placed on boards and superintendents to modify and develop programs and policies and deliver adequate economic resources to provide students with a quality education.

As instructors in advanced degree programs in educational leadership at two institutions of higher education in Wisconsin, we (the editors) were hearing concerns about the pace of change and complaints about initiative fatigue over and over from our graduate students (mostly current teachers and administrators), practicing school administrators, and board members. What we heard was an articulation of the need to address these issues.

We also heard about the practical and human elements of addressing PK–12 students' needs while learning about and developing ways to successfully implement all of the initiatives described and more.

While change creates opportunities, it also creates urgency, stress, the need for communication, the need for learning, and the need to address the complexity of how the changes affect school governance. Frankly, on a personal level, we were dismayed by an apparent rise in early retirements of educators and a high level of agitation from those who couldn't retire early.

Our contributing authors have firsthand knowledge based on practical experience and theoretical underpinnings. Most of these individuals are current practitioners, and they have gone above and beyond the call of duty by giving their time, knowledge, and thoughtful reflection to share with readers. We believe these insights, intended for a uniquely mixed audience of both board members and superintendents, can enhance board and superintendent relationships, partnerships, and interactions.

BOARD/SUPERINTENDENT INTERACTIONS

1

ISSUES, CONTEXTS, AND FRAMEWORKS

Amy E. Van Deuren and Thomas F. Evert

Today's educational landscape is marked by complex issues related to a challenging national economic recovery, increasing demands for accountability, and a variety of educational options, including charter schools, choice schools, and online schools. In addition, the foundational structure of schools is changing as many question the appropriateness of the traditional "factory model" of schooling, in which children are educated in batches according to their birth year.

School board/superintendent relationships are more important than ever as these leadership teams grapple with the demands placed on their districts from state and federal governments and their own communities. While it is true that the educational landscape is changing, individual school districts must align in some agreeable manner with the communities that they serve. This work is challenging indeed as board/superintendent teams work through many changes, issue by issue, over time.

The authority conferred to local school boards matters. School boards set tax levies, approve staffing hires, make policy, hire the superintendent, and perform a number of other specific legal responsibilities articulated in statutes. The manner in which board members conduct business and interact among themselves, with the superintendent, and with the public sets the tone for the direction and success of the district.

The board does not work in a vacuum; it is the interaction or relationship between the board and superintendent that ultimately sets the stage for success or tension in the district. When the board/superintendent partnership works successfully, both entities understand state and federal mandates as well as a multitude of issues including curriculum, instruction, staffing, budgeting, operations, and, most importantly, student achievement. Both entities understand the community in which they live and work, and they understand the ways that public education reflects the values of today while preparing students for the world of tomorrow.

The information presented in this chapter is intended to connect the dots for readers by providing general frameworks for consideration that illustrate some of the complexity of issues faced by boards and superintendents in today's educational landscape. The book is organized into three main sections dealing with three key areas representing significant issues: (1) contexts and frameworks, (2) insights and tools to address current key issues in education, and (3) resources that may assist in addressing issues.

Part I comprises this chapter. It provides overarching frameworks to structure board/superintendent content, connectivity (communication and relationships), and relevance. Other material in this book may be layered with the frameworks provided in this chapter.

The current issues addressed in this book are not intended to be exhaustive; instead, the chapters on current issues in part II provide details and tools that serve as timely examples of the ways that school districts are thinking about and/or working through these issues. These chapters can help readers identify what types of information, tools, and resources may be helpful as they work through their own issues of the day, whether those issues are the same or different than those presented in this work.

Finally, it is important that both school boards and superintendents have access to quality resources that can provide them with information and guidance. Part III of the book provides resources that can be used by both school boards and superintendents to obtain more information on a variety of relevant issues.

The resources, tools, and examples of applying the frameworks are useful and demonstrate their applicability to a wide variety of challenges and opportunities boards and superintendents face daily. We believe this book is a valuable resource for boards and superintendents, not only for the content contained in it, but, perhaps more importantly, as a starting point for open and productive dialogue between boards and superintendents.

FRAMEWORK I: STATE AND NATIONAL CONTEXTS

It is no wonder that school boards and superintendents are sometimes at odds in today's educational landscape; it has been decades in the making. In *A Nation At Risk* (1983), the report of the National Commission on Excellence in Education engaged in new levels of criticism about the quality of education offered in America's public schools and made specific recommendations for improvement. "The report propelled a move from measuring school quality by resources received and onto a plane where performance is judged on outcomes students achieve" (Guthrie and Springer, 2004, p. 7). *A Nation at Risk* fueled the increase of the federal government's involvement in education, and education reform emanating from the federal government increased steadily throughout the 1980s and 1990s.

The 1990s were marked by increased pressure on public schools to stress curriculum standards, student achievement, and standardized testing. These trends were reflected in the 1994 reauthorization of the Elementary and Secondary Education Act (ESEA), called the Improving America's Schools Act (IASA), which was marked by adding standards for assessment to provide accountability for student achievement.

This push for accountability was the result of national politicians, including Bill Clinton, George W. Bush, and Ted Kennedy, calling for more federal involvement in education and higher student achievement throughout the nation as reflected in standardized test scores. However, it was not until the passage of the No Child Left Behind Act of 2001 (NCLB) that accountability for student achievement through standardized testing became a full-scale reality.

The 1990s were also marked by the beginnings of changes that are part of our educational fabric today, including school vouchers and charter schools. In 1990, Milwaukee Public Schools survived legal challenges to offer the Milwaukee Parental Choice Program, providing state-paid vouchers for tuition, enabling low-income students to attend private schools in Milwaukee (Ritsche, 2001). In 1991, Minnesota was the first state to legislate charter schools. Arkansas governor Bill Clinton supported the charter school movement on a national level during this time in office.

The first decade of the twenty-first century was marked by a dramatic national economic downturn that had a significant impact on education as funding to public schools markedly declined. In 2009, Race to the Top funding was introduced as part of the American Recovery and Reinvestment Act (ARRA). This federal legislation resulted in many states changing state legislation and policies to become competitive for the federal funds, and also accelerated the push toward Common Core State Standards, a critical component for Race to the Top funding.

Today, the charter school movement continues to grow and other alternatives for school choice are more readily available than ever before (for example, open enrollment and online schools). While these options provide viable alternatives for many students, issues surrounding funding and the effects of funneling public education dollars to these educational alternatives on public schools continue to be experienced and debated.

Currently, boards and superintendents face many pressures as a result of the educational landscape and economic climate. Many states continue to reduce funding for education while demands for demonstrating increased student achievement and staff accountability at all levels continue to rise. Demands for increased technological capacity require regular updates to district infrastructures. Many districts are experiencing increases in the number of students in poverty and in the number of students qualifying for special education services. At the same time, many of these districts are also experiencing decreases in support staff, administration, and teachers as they try to do more with less.

School boards and superintendents have been tasked with raising test scores and demanding that school personnel be held accountable for student learning. In many states, they have been given this task in an environment of decreased state funding and a tax-weary local public. School board members are asked to make critical decisions about finances, budgets, tax rates, and policy direction, and they rely on the superintendent to guide them through making these high-stakes decisions.

It is important that school boards and superintendents understand and acknowledge state and federal contexts because they have an enormous impact on how schools are run and how students are taught in today's public schools. As boards and superintendents work together to operate within these contexts, while also looking for new and creative ways to improve student achievement and maximize resources, the strength and effectiveness of the board/superintendent relationship becomes more important than ever.

A deep knowledge base is required by boards and superintendents to balance legal requirements with community values and interests inherent in both the board and superintendent positions. It is finding this balance and continuing to search for better ways to educate our children that ultimately results in a successful board/superintendent partnership and a successful school district.

FRAMEWORK 2: TIMELINESS AND RELEVANCY—THE ISSUES OF TODAY, TOMORROW, AND ALWAYS

In any discussion of school district leadership, it is worth discussing the issue of timeliness. That is, board/superintendent teams address issues that are both specific to the day and age in which they serve in their leadership roles, and issues that remain relatively constant over time. For example, setting tax levies, budgeting, and resource allocation are all issues that have been part and parcel of board/superintendent work for decades, and will likely remain so into the foreseeable future. On the other hand, issues such as mainstreaming, open classrooms, Response to Intervention (RTI), Common Core State Standards, and inclusion are issues specific to an era.

Each wave of new educational initiatives and trends brings its own lexicon and detail; yet as anyone who has a lengthy involvement in education can attest, "new" ideas and trends have a great deal in common with ideas and trends of the past. Recognizing the timeliness or timelessness of certain issues can keep experienced board members and

Timelessness	Timeliness
• Tax Levies	• Curriculum programming
• Budgets	• School- and district-wide initiatives
• Staffing	• New legislative state and federal mandates
• Collective Bargaining or Teacher Compensation	• Use of technology
• Facilities Management	• Specific examples include: RtI, Common Core State Standards, Teacher Evaluation Systems, Alternative Teacher Compensation Models
• The fact of legislative mandates	
• Political/legislative advocacy	
• Accountability to Public	

Figure 1.1. Timelessness and Timeliness: Issues Facing Boards and Superintendents

superintendents from falling into patterns of stagnation that can occur when relying solely on past experience.

Figure 1.1 illustrates the ways that issues in public education can be generally divided into categories of timelessness and timeliness. Of course, even issues that are considered for this exercise as "timeless" are contextualized in current political and economic climates; the criteria for categorization rests in the knowledge base necessary to engage in analysis and decision making on the topic.

Figure 1.1 illustrates certain issues likely to remain consistent over time in terms of what a board member or superintendent needs to know to engage in analysis and decision making. The terminology and basic structure of the items in the left-hand column stay steady over time. Indeed, many board members and superintendents can serve long and successful tenures in their positions with a single foundational knowledge base in these areas.

The items in the right-hand column are a different story. These issues of timeliness often require a steep learning curve and are those issues that the board and superintendent must often act on quickly. Sometimes the issue is not about board choice, but rather about legal compliance. Other times there are several options that a school district

ISSUES, CONTEXTS, AND FRAMEWORKS

can adopt, and it is up to the board to ultimately decide which specific implementations they will use. These decisions can impact school districts for years, and reflect the ways that vision and goals are manifested in educational practice.

Considering various responsibilities of the board/superintendent team in terms of timelessness and timeliness can help focus board professional development. New board members are likely to need more orientation on the timeless issues so that they can establish a foundation of knowledge that they can build upon with experience throughout their time of service. Seasoned board members may want refreshers on these timeless issues and are likely to be more interested in learning about current issues of timeliness so that they stay up to date and remain knowledgeable about current educational trends.

SUMMARY

The three sections of this book address issues of high relevance to board/superintendent teams, including current issues in education and resources. Two primary frameworks are provided to give readers a variety of contextual references to facilitate understanding and discussion: (1) consideration of state and national contexts and (2) consideration of timeliness and relevancy.

State and national contexts provide the underpinnings for public school governance. As boards and superintendents work through issues of import in their districts, understanding that nothing happens in a vacuum is critical; that is, all districts are subject to state and national laws and regulations that frame everything public schools do, from curriculum and testing to facilities and operations.

Boards and superintendents are wise to gain an understanding of the nature of the issues that they are addressing. Some issues are ongoing and have been part of school district governance for a long time, while others are the results of new tools, technologies, and/or social conventions. Understanding the past while identifying present issues and future trends can help boards and superintendents prioritize issues and actions to effectively maximize and manage district resources for student learning.

REFERENCES

Guthrie, J. W., and Springer, M. G. (2004). *A Nation at Risk* revisited: Did "wrong" reasoning result in "right" results? At what cost? *Peabody Journal of Education* 79(1), 7–35.

The National Commission on Excellence in Education (1983). *A Nation at Risk: The imperative for educational reform.* Washington, DC: U.S. Department of Education

Ritsche, D. (2001). Wisconsin Briefs from the Legislative Reference Bureau. LRB-01-WB-4, January 2001.

BOARDS AND SUPERINTENDENTS ADDRESS CURRENT ISSUES TOGETHER

UNDERSTANDING THE COMPREHENSIVE CURRICULUM PROCESS

Linda Nortier

KEY ISSUES FOR BOARD MEMBERS AND SUPERINTENDENTS

I would like to propose an integrated view of curriculum development as a focal point for realizing a district's mission and vision. While the district superintendent and the school board are rarely involved in the work of developing, implementing, and assessing curriculum, they assist by developing the mission and vision in a strategic/long-range plan. A successful Comprehensive Curriculum Process involves the integration and interaction of four key elements that inform one another.

Element Integration for Continuous Learning. Figure 2.1 illustrates the elements of a Comprehensive Curriculum Process that, when understood as interactive, drive district activity toward a coherent whole with a focus on continuous learning improvement for staff, administration, and students.

The graphic is a group of overlapping circles, intended to convey the flexibility and the connective, integrated thinking required to create a comprehensive curriculum process. The process describes the teaching and learning elements that are necessary in a district for a cohesive and directed focus on student learning. The starting point for the process

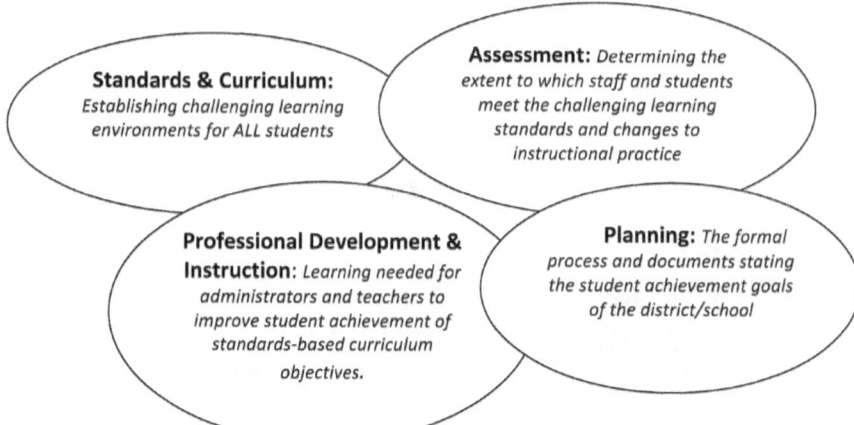

Figure 2.1. Four Elements of a Comprehensive Curriculum Process

is based on the individual district priorities rather than an artificially imposed template.

Elements and Questions. These four elements of a comprehensive curriculum process echo the four questions that DuFour, DuFour, and Eaker (2008) posit as the foundation of a learning environment. The specific questions posed when determining the extent to which a curriculum may be comprehensive were:

1. What should students know and be able to do? (Standards and curriculum);
2. How will we know they can do it? (Assessments);
3. How will we ensure that all students meet the curriculum standards? (Planning);
4. What will we do if they can't or don't already know how? (Professional development and instruction).

DuFour and colleagues' questions help define the elements of the Comprehensive Curriculum Process. However, they need more clarity if they are to be useful in practice. The rest of this chapter is focused on unpacking each of the four elements of the Comprehensive Curriculum Process.

Element 1: Standards and Curriculum

Within curriculum plans, a clear connection between standards and the specific application of performance objectives must be evident. The content of each course is clearly stated in high-level objectives (Marzano, 2009; Reeves, 2010) and aligned to standards, which provide the foundation for curriculum-based assessments.

The Superintendent's View of Standards and Curriculum. Superintendents are not necessarily involved in the hands-on work of curriculum, but are responsible for oversight and coordination of curriculum implementation. The superintendency is difficult enough, with a plethora of people and issues demanding attention. Table 2.1 provides guiding questions that superintendents may ask to deepen understanding of curriculum development processes used by staff. A "Listen For" section is presented alongside each question to help in the analysis of responses.

The data gathered from these questions can help guide district-level decision making on curriculum-related issues. While the components of the curriculum process are not sequential, the documentation of curriculum work is likely the most appropriate place to start.

Figure 2.2. Standards and Curriculum

Table 2.1. Questions and "Listen Fors" Related to Standards and Curriculum—Superintendent

Questions about Standards and Curriculum	Listen For:
What design for curriculum development was used?	• Researched designs
	• Criteria for selection
How was the design of the curriculum chosen?	• Educator response to the design
What is the location and accessibility of the documents themselves?	• Participants in development of the documentation
• How broad-based was representation on the development committee?	• Concerns about the process and implementation
• Have there been concerns or issues generated in the curriculum development process?	○ How are concerns stated?
	○ What concerns have already been addressed?
	○ What are the outcomes of the concerns addressed?
Does the curriculum document assist students in meeting the standards?	• Objectives of the curriculum units are written in higher-level verbs (Forehand, 2012)
	• Direct alignment from the unit objectives to the standards
	• Stated assessments are designed to assess the objectives
	• Assistance in supporting all students in the content is evident
	• Curriculum document is directly linked to instruction
How was the curriculum documentation introduced to teachers not directly involved in the development process?	• Ongoing support for continued development of teacher content knowledge
What evidence do we have that the documents are used to guide instruction?	• Number of teachers suggesting modifications
	• Requests for materials to support the instruction outlined in the documents
	• The curriculum implementation is directly linked to educator evaluation process
How are the documents revised?	• Person directly responsible for monitoring revisions and how the process is ongoing
	• Frequency and/or engagement in revisions
How are the documents accessed?	• Curriculum documents are no longer in paper form
	• Documents are centrally accessed with assessments and data collection formats linked
	• All teachers review the processes of curriculum implementation

The conversations with board members, administrators, teachers, and parents concerning these responses and evidence provide the superintendent with direction for addressing the areas of assessment, planning, and professional development and instruction.

A School Board Member's View of Standards and Curriculum. While school board members are elected to support student learning and achievement, they are even further removed from the curriculum development process than the superintendent. However, board members are responsible to the community for student success and have an implied duty to understand how curriculum influences that success. School board members receive standards and curriculum information in a variety of ways. First, new courses for the district are typically proposed to the board for approval. Second, major revisions to current curriculum are completed and usually require only board review. Finally, boards may reference standards and curriculum when achievement data are presented or made public.

Given the components of the standards and curriculum element, board members may be informed by the set of questions presented in table 2.2. As with the previous set of questions, they are followed by "Listen Fors" (as are all questions presented for each of the four elements) that can be used to aid in the analysis of responses.

As board members responsible for the overall success of students, these questions represent district-level insights on student learning and achievement at the board level. Responses to these questions may provide insight into the best ways to allocate district resources to maximize curriculum effectiveness. Asking relevant questions informs board members about efforts to improve student learning.

Table 2.2. Questions and "Listen Fors" Related to Standards and Curriculum—School Board

Questions about Standards and Curriculum	Listen For:

New Course curriculum:
• How will this course help more students achieve the standards?
• What data will be collected to document student achievement of the standards?
• What is the projected impact on existing courses?
	• Currently students are struggling with . . .
	• Currently more students have already met the standards of the current courses offered . . .
	• This course reaches students who . . .
	• More students will be prepared for . . .
	• Data will include:
	  ○ Standardized tests
	  ○ Curriculum-based data
	  ○ Enrollments
	  ○ Grade distribution

Curriculum Revision to update with new standards: • How will this curriculum be implemented? • What will teachers need to be able to implement the curriculum? • What data will be collected to demonstrate success?	• Meeting new state requirements • Remaining ahead of the "curve" • Teachers involved in the development process • Assessments documented in the curriculum
Achievement Data presentation: • Do the data findings reflect what our curriculum documents contain? • Are there necessary revisions to the curriculum that these data suggest?	• Comparison to district-based achievement data • Discrepancies suggest . . . • We will . . . • We are celebrating . . . • We need to work on . . .

Element 2: Assessment

The value of a specific content curriculum is evaluated on the evidence of student learning (assessment). Teacher, student, parent, and administrator knowledge of acceptable evidence of learning must be clear and documented through multiple methods within the curriculum plans. Further, the intended use of the results should be determined before any assessment is implemented.

Arguably, the design and implementation of assessments is the most challenging aspect of curriculum development. Both internal teacher-made or curriculum-provided assessments and external state-imposed assessments provide different and important evidence of learning out-

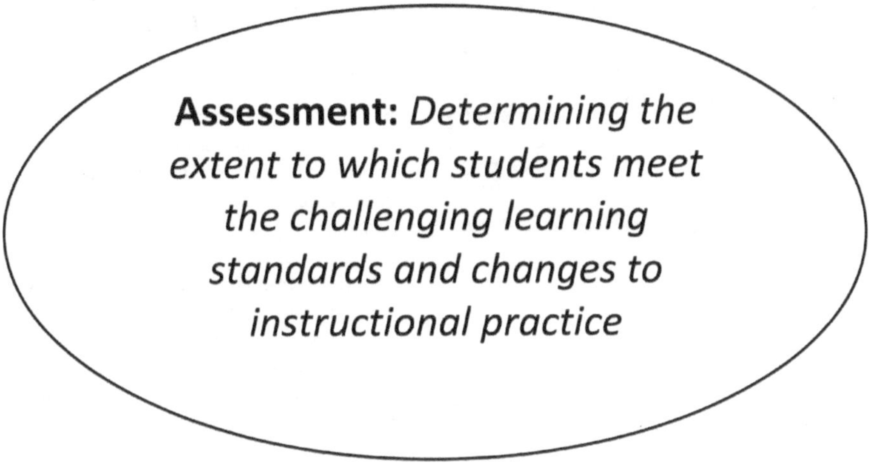

> **Assessment:** *Determining the extent to which students meet the challenging learning standards and changes to instructional practice*

Figure 2.3. Assessment

comes. If curriculum plans are well designed and meet the established criteria and standards, leaders should pay attention to the student learning that results from both internal and external assessments.

Superintendent's View of Assessment. Superintendents seek to cultivate and build human capacity throughout the district. Developing curriculum-based assessments provides the professional learning opportunity to build a foundation of assessment literacy (Popham, 2003; 2009). Teachers and administrators must become critical consumers of assessment design and data. The answers to the questions in table 2.3 may assist in determining the district's level of assessment literacy. Table 2.3 provides questions and "Listen Fors" that superintendents can use to determine the amount and type of assessments used in the district.

The School Board View of Assessment. School board members who find assessment data reported in the news as simple comparisons of school districts are viewing their districts in superficial terms. While there are many questions to ask about what the data actually represent in terms of student achievement, school board members want to know how assessments are used to drive improvement of student learning. The implications of responses should open discussions regarding what administrators, staff, students, and parents need to know about assessment. Table 2.4 provides questions and "Listen Fors" that board members can use to determine the amount and type of assessments used in the district.

Table 2.3. Questions and "Listen Fors" Related to Assessment—Superintendent

Questions about Assessment	Listen For:
• Are there curriculum-based assessments?	• Hopefully you will hear that there is a comprehensive system of curriculum-based student assessments that are directly tied to the curriculum documents.
• What guide materials were used to design the assessments?	• Teachers and administrators should be able to describe the research process for acceptable models and the current state and national design requirements for standards assessment.
• How faithfully implemented are the curriculum-based assessments? • How are the data from the implementation of these assessments aggregated? • How are the data from the curriculum-based assessments used?	• Administrators and team leaders should be able to discuss how the assessments are implemented and the data are collected. • Examples of the curriculum-based assessment data reports should be available. • Administrators and teachers should be able to describe the outcomes of the assessments and trends of student learning based on these assessments.
• What district-chosen standardized assessments are used? How often are they implemented? What do they tell us about student learning?	• Relationship of assessments to the actual curriculum/instruction. • Analysis of time given to assessments and relationship to data applications to modified instruction.
• What instructional and professional learning changes have been made based on the combined data?	• Opportunities for teachers and administrators to regularly review data and instructional practice. • These opportunities should also generate plans for the next stages of professional learning.
• How are data used to evaluate program effectiveness?	• Programs and initiatives that are recommended for continuance or extinction based on data should be a general component of assessment discussions.
• What is the school board's understanding and attitude concerning assessment?	• The school board's response to assessment information will reveal the level of understanding and attitude of board members. • (This may help to suggest the types of learning activities you need to provide for the board.)

UNDERSTANDING THE COMPREHENSIVE CURRICULUM PROCESS

Table 2.4. Questions and "Listen Fors" Related to Assessment—School Board

Questions about Assessment	Listen For:
• Beyond the scores listed in the newspaper, what assessment data are available to teachers and administrators? • How does this data inform students and parents about student achievement?	• Beyond merely a list of standardized assessments, staff should be able to explain why the assessment is necessary so that they are able to respond to student learning needs. • The reporting of data to students and parents should be understandable. The information should provide guidance in the use of the data and why it is important for students' next steps. An example might include "given this score, you may be eligible for extra assistance in math. See your guidance counselor to sign up."

• What else should teachers and administrators know about assessment?	• Teachers and administrators discussing the specific elements of assessment literacy (W. James Popham, 2009). Some specific topics to hear included:
	  ○ Design of assessments, standardized and curriculum based.
	  ○ Student involvement in understanding and implementation of assessments.
	  ○ Preparation of students for various types of testing.
	  ○ Criteria for student success and implications of failure.

• How are parents informed of student achievement overall?	• Discussion of reporting systems including report cards and how student achievement information is structured. • The relationship among all forms of student reports.
• What do parents need to know about the current state of student assessments?	• Parents should receive an overview of assessment development. Their information and opinions concerning assessment generally evolve from their own experience. Communications from the district need to be clear and concise.

Element 3: Planning

The key to effective planning for improved student achievement is the intentional link of the four elements of the Comprehensive Curriculum Process. That is, planning is the engine that drives the process, and the resulting plan is the infrastructure that forms the foundation of the Comprehensive Curriculum Process. Creating short- and long-term goals in strategic/long-range planning using all elements of the Comprehensive Curriculum Process will also support a continuous improvement model.

Superintendent's View of Planning. Planning in the pure Comprehensive Curriculum Process model refers specifically to curriculum development; however, superintendents rarely engage directly with curriculum. Instead, district leaders are primarily concerned with setting long- and short-term goals through a strategic planning process.

In the interest of presenting contextually relevant information, the questions and "Listen Fors" presented in table 2.5 reflect the strategic planning process, which is critically, if somewhat indirectly, tied to curriculum development.

Evaluating the effectiveness of a district's strategic/long-range planning is a rather complex process. Identifying who or what is missing from the plan is just as important as what is actually contained in it. Documentation and implementation of the four elements may assist

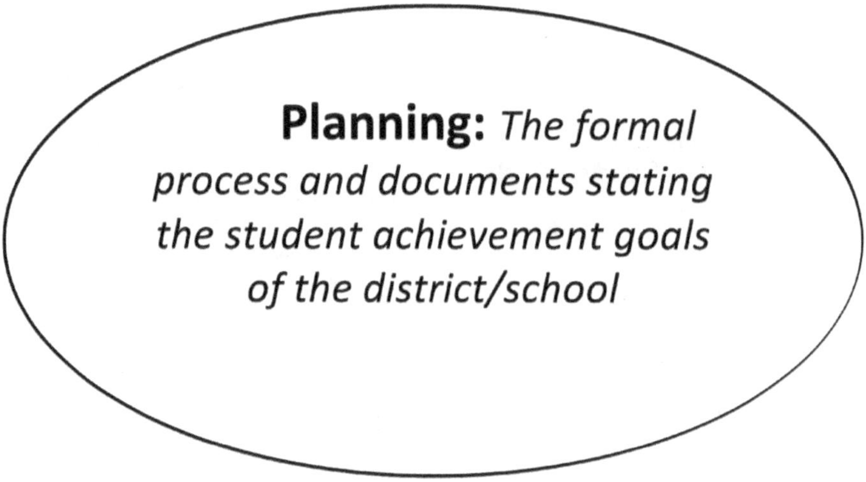

Planning: *The formal process and documents stating the student achievement goals of the district/school*

Figure 2.4. Planning

UNDERSTANDING THE COMPREHENSIVE CURRICULUM PROCESS

Table 2.5. Questions and "Listen Fors" Related to Planning—Superintendent

Questions about Planning	Listen For:
• How is future planning documented? • How are documents developed and who participates? • How are the documents used once they are developed?	• A straightforward plan format that documents a long-range vision. • Participation of all staff in the development of goals and strategies. • Link to curriculum, assessment, student and staff learning.
• Allocation of time to thoughtful planning.	• Importance of analysis and collegial discussion in planning. • Engagement of school staff, board members, community, and students.
• What is missing from the documents?	• Elements or targets for staff, students, and operations that should be impacted by a comprehensive plan.
• How are teacher and administrator evaluations directly linked to the long-range plan? • How are professional development activities determined?	• Development of professional learning plans based on the student learning needs. • Staff evaluation process that encompasses student and staff learning. • How professional learning opportunities support differentiated learning needs of staff.

superintendents in developing a firm foundation and understanding of curriculum development.

School Board Members' View of Planning. School board members must have a firm grasp of the district's mission, vision, and goals. A well-conceived strategic/long-range plan written in specific terms and language will assist board members when deciding whether or not to support individual actions and policies. Table 2.6 provides questions and "Listen Fors" related to strategic/long-range planning that may be useful for boards.

Each board member should expect to be involved in the development or ongoing revision of the district's long-range plan. Straightforward language that is clear to all constituents is an important component of communicating an effective plan. Board members should look for alignment among the mission, vision, and goals embedded in the long-range plan and new activities and policies that come up for board consideration and approval.

Planning for Boards and Superintendents. Figure 2.5 presents a simple tool for engaging in a systems-focused strategic/long-range planning process.

Table 2.6. Questions and "Listen Fors" Related to Planning—School Board

Questions about Planning	Listen For:

• What are the main goals of the plan that help guide school board actions?	• Specific goals that impact all areas of school operations:
	  ○ Professional learning needs based on student learning needs.
	  ○ Purchasing to support staff and students.
	  ○ Policy decisions that support changes in operations.
	  ○ Acceptable evidence of success.

• How are goals and activities interconnected?	• Activities are well defined with responsibilities assigned. • Logical connections of each activity to the curriculum elements.
• How is the plan used to guide school board decisions?	• References (actually pulling out the plan) to the plan frequently as difficult decisions are discussed at the board level.
• Can the plan be read and understood by noneducators of the community?	• Language used is descriptive and accurate interpretation of the plan's intent is clear.

	Public Engagement	Academic Standards	Curriculum/ Instruction	Assessment	Equity	Professional Development	Connection to Higher Ed.
Perspectives: What concerns, questions, or worries do we have about professional learning?	•	•	•	•	•	•	•
Vision: What would we see going on if we had the perfect professional learning organization within the district?	•	•	•	•	•	•	•
Evidence: What would be the evidence that professional learning activities are helping teachers and students learn?	•	•	•	•	•	•	•
Activities: What will we have to do to reach the vision and provide the evidence necessary?	•	•	•	•	•	•	•
Barriers/Questions: What gets in the way of reaching the vision? What questions need to be answered?	•	•	•	•	•	•	•
Change: What do we need to do to overcome the barriers?	•	•	•	•	•	•	•

Figure 2.5. Strategic/Long-Range Planning Questions—Superintendent and School Board. Adapted from Education Commission of the States (ECS, 1998), Stages of Implementation of Standards-Led Education

UNDERSTANDING THE COMPREHENSIVE CURRICULUM PROCESS

The framework itself is important, as are the conversations that arise as a result of engaging a variety of stakeholders in this process. Dialogues concerning the future of the district using a systems process are much more likely to produce divergent thinking leading to more forward-thinking and effective strategic/long-range plans. Senge (1994) recommends that strategic/long-term planning processes result in not more than four to six goal areas.

When considering district goals, Golarz and Golarz (1995) recommend that the board set the direction for the "what" of goal setting, while the superintendent, administration, and staff are responsible for the "how" that leads to achieving these goals.

Element 4: Professional Development and Instruction

Professional development refers to the learning opportunities provided either directly or indirectly by the district, based on the strategic/long-range plan and designed to build staff capacity in the development and delivery of instruction. When this element of a Comprehensive Curriculum Plan is linked to the other three elements, it increases the

Figure 2.6. Professional Development & Instruction

synergy of the other elements. The development of a professional learning plan as a foundation for district improvement includes the directions and processes identified within the other three elements of a Comprehensive Curriculum Plan.

Superintendent's View of Professional Development and Instruction. Leadership of the district's professional learning opportunities so that they result in improved student learning is a comprehensive task. Staff support is critical to the success of any strategic/long-range plan. Development of the district's strategic/long-range plan sets the tone for cooperative and unique options for the design of professional learning opportunities (Darling-Hammond, 2006a).

Table 2.7 presents questions critical in designing appropriate structures that will facilitate the necessary learning to enhance professional practice (instruction).

The Board Member's View of Professional Development and Instruction. The school board's responsibility in professional development and the improvement of instruction should focus on the successful implementation of the goals embedded in the strategic/long-range plan. Table 2.8 provides guiding questions that may help boards better understand

Table 2.7. Questions and "Listen Fors" Related to Professional Development & Instruction—Superintendent

Questions about Professional Development and Instruction	Listen For:
• How are teacher and administrator evaluations linked to professional learning?	• There should be a specific process of connecting student learning to professional learning and the opportunities to learn.
• What are the district and school resources that support professional learning?	• Scheduling of days devoted to professional learning.
• What elements of the educator contacts support continuous professional learning?	• How the days of professional learning are organized to support the individual learning needs of staff.
• What constitutes movement on the salary scale and district recognitions of advancement?	• The recognition of learning in the contractual agreements.
	• How departments, schools, or collegial teams organize their learning options.
• What is the school board's attitude toward professional learning?	• Responsibility for learning.
	• Willingness to consider alternative plans for professional learning.
	• Extending contracts.

Table 2.8. Questions and "Listen Fors" Related to Professional Development & Instruction—School Board

Questions about Professional Development and Instruction	Listen For:
• How are professional learning opportunities designed?	• Link to long-range planning. • Link to assessments. • Collegial development.
• How is the effectiveness of professional learning evaluated?	• Direct links established between student learning goals, programming, and professional learning activities.
• Current professional learning activities and future or ideal activities envisioned.	• The continuous link from current to future activities.

the context and processes of professional development as it relates to the quality of instruction.

SUMMARY

Curriculum development and implementation is not an isolated activity separate from the overarching goals of the district. In answering DuFour's four critical questions for which we are all responsible, the elements of curriculum development become inseparable and guide our search for answers to the critical questions both school superintendents and the school boards should ask.

There is no sequence in which a district must address the four elements of the Comprehensive Curriculum Process. Instead, it is the answers to the questions that are asked that help determine where the process should begin. While these four elements were presented separately, it is the integration of these elements that determines the most effective implementation for curriculum development for any given school district. Using the questions in the tables, board members and superintendents can ascertain significant information and determine entry points into the Comprehensive Curriculum Process that will deliver the greatest initial and long-term success.

ADDITIONAL MATERIALS

Superintendent's and Board Member's Overview of Standards-Based Curriculum Involvement in a Complex Process

Professional development and instruction: Learning needed for administrators and teachers to improve student achievement of standards-based curriculum objectives.

- Use of the curriculum development process to identify and create teacher-directed learning opportunities based on deepening content and instructional practice knowledge.
- Time and alternatives provided for teacher work.
- Instructional models, strategies, and tools.

Planning: The formal process and documents stating the student achievement goals of the district/school.

- School improvement plan format focused on clear goals of student learning.
- Educator effectiveness framework focused on student learning goals.
- Use of data to inform school and educator improvement planning.
- Plan results communicated to staff and public.

Standards and curriculum: Establishing challenging learning environments for ALL students.

- Documents demonstrate alignment from classroom practice to achievement of the standards.
- Align district curriculum and instruction to the Common Core State Standards.
- All teachers understand the application of the standards to all content areas.
- All teachers can describe their content in terms of its disciplinary literacy.
- Emphasis is on ALL students achieving the standards.

Assessment: Determining the extent to which staff and students meet the challenging learning standards and changes to instructional practice.

- Internal and external data collection.
- Process of data analysis.
- Reporting process.
- School and classroom curriculum-based assessments with data aggregated and analyzed.
- District assessment plan designed to integrate assessment data.

Ask all the right questions:

- How do we document what students should know and be able to do?
- How do we know what they've learned?
- What's the backup plan if they don't learn?
- How are our teachers prepared to continuously learn?
- How are we moving to the future?
- How do we establish priorities?

REFERENCES

Argyris, C. (1991). Teaching smart people how to learn. *Harvard Business Review* 69(3), 99–109.

Clay, M. V., and Soldwedel, P. (2008). *How to encourage school board accountability*. Bloomington, IN: Solution Tree Press.

Dalal, A. D. (2008). *School implementation of a board-adopted inquiry process to improve student learning*. Unpublished EdD, University of California, San Diego, California.

Darling-Hammond, L. (1998). Teachers and teaching: Testing policy hypotheses from a national commission report. *Educational Researcher* 27(1), 5–15.

Darling-Hammond, L. (2006a). *Powerful teacher education: Lessons from exemplary programs*. San Francisco: Jossey-Bass.

Darling-Hammond, L. (2006b). Securing the right to learn: Policy and practice for powerful teaching and learning. *Educational Researcher* 35(7), 13–24.

Darling-Hammond, L., and Youngs, P. (2002). Defining "highly qualified teachers": What does "scientifically-based research" actually tell us? *Educational Researcher* 31(9), 13–25.

D'Orio, W. (2002). Holding school boards more accountable. *District Administration*. Norwalk, CT: Association of Educational Administrators.

DuFour, R., DuFour, R., and Eaker R. (2008). *Revisiting professional learning communities at work*. Bloomington, IN: Solution Tree.

ECS. (1998). *Stages of implementation of standards led education*. Denver, CO: Education Commission of the States.

Forehand, M. (2012). Bloom's Taxonomy. *Emerging perspectives on learning, teaching and technology*. Retrieved from http://epltt.coe.uga.edu/index.php?title=Bloom%27s_Taxonomy.

Golarz, R., and Golarz, M. (1995). *The power of participation: Improving schools in a democratic society*. Champaign, IL: Research Press.

Marzano, R. J. (2009). *Formative assessment and standards-based grading: Classroom strategies that work*. Bloomington, IN: Solution Tree.

McAdams, D. R. (2008). Getting your board out of micromanagement. *The School Administrator* 65(10). Retrieved from www.aasa.org.

McTighe, J., and Wiggins, G. (1999). *The understanding by design handbook*. Alexandria, VA: Association for Supervision and Curriculum Development.

Munson, L., Wells, C., Stern, R., and Griffith, L. (2012). *Common core curriculum maps in English language arts*. San Francisco: Jossey-Bass.

Popham, W. J. (2003). *Assessment for educational leaders*. Boston: Pearson.

Popham, W. J. (2009). Assessment literacy for teachers: Faddish or fundamental? *Theory into Practice* 48(1), 4–11.

Reeves, D. (2010). *Elements of grading: A guide to effective practice*. Bloomington, IN: Solution Tree Press.

Rothstein, D., and Santana, L. (2011). Teaching students to ask their own questions. *Harvard Education Letter* 27(5). This item came off the Internet at this location: http://hepg.org/hel-home/issues/27_5/helarticle/teaching-students-to-ask-their-own-questions_507#home.

Senge, P. (1994). *The fifth discipline*. New York: Doubleday.

Wiggins, G. (2005). *The Understanding by Design guide to creating high-quality units*. Alexandria, VA: Association for Supervision and Curriculum Development.

Wiggins, G., and McTighe, J. (2012). *The Understanding by Design Guide to advanced concepts in creating and reviewing units*. Alexandria, VA: Association for Supervision and Curriculum Development.

COMPREHENSIVE STUDENT SUPPORT SYSTEMS AS EXEMPLIFIED BY RTI

A District Report for Boards and Superintendents
Denise L. Wellnitz and Thomas F. Evert

Federal and state laws have formalized the obligations of boards and superintendents to address the needs of all students. Clear moral, legal, ethical, and financial reasons to provide a quality education for every learner are well documented. These reasons exist regardless of whether a student has an Individual Education Program (IEP), is identified as an at-risk learner, or qualifies as an English Language Learner (ELL).

State and federal governments have mandated that public schools educate all students in prekindergarten through twelfth grade. Over the past five years, new mandates have resulted in an approach wherein multiple services are provided at varying levels to address the learning needs of each student. The mechanisms to achieve the goals of these mandates have been generally described as student learning support systems.

In terms of background, and for board members and superintendents and those readers wanting a comprehensive and academic understanding of addressing student needs, the work of Dr. Howard Adelman and Dr. Linda Taylor, co-leaders of the UCLA National Center for Mental Health in School, provides an important foundation. The center has been in existence since 1986 and has provided school districts with a systemic model for addressing comprehensive methods to develop and enhance student learning support systems.

In 2008, Adelman and Taylor joined forces with Scholastic to address unique student learning needs in southern states where Hurricane Katrina ravaged families and schools in 2005. The demanding circumstances created by Katrina, coupled with the partnership of Scholastic and the UCLA Center, resulted in the Rebuilding for Learning Initiative. This initiative focused on the development of goals for student growth, the use of a model to enhance communication, and the development of materials to enhance student services provided at the district level.

Adelman and Taylor (2004, 2011) also provided in-depth policy, procedural, and systemic plans to address ways to capture the interest and commitment of board members and superintendents in developing and implementing comprehensive student learning support systems. These articles address school board involvement and the superintendent's role at the district level. They provide in-depth analysis of the need for purposeful planning at the highest levels of leadership in the area of student learning support systems.

Mapping and managing resources is one of the processes provided by Adelman and Taylor (2006b) to address barriers to learning. They produced a technical packet titled *Resource Management and Mapping to Address Barriers to Learning: An Intervention for Systemic Change*. This packet details the functions and tasks and provides a rubric of the mapping and the managing resources process a district and community can use to take stock of the resources already being expended and consider how these resources can be used to the greatest effect.

This chapter presents an analysis of how one district has addressed and continues to utilize a comprehensive student learning support system broadly based on the work of Adelman and Taylor. The analysis in this chapter focuses on students who are considered at-risk learners. The analysis is written from one author's perspective (Dr. Wellnitz) as a superintendent who has served for five years in a rural Wisconsin school district of over eight hundred students.

ANALYSIS OF STUDENT LEARNING SUPPORT SYSTEMS IN A RURAL SCHOOL DISTRICT

History and Implementation of Comprehensive Student Support System. The Darlington Community School District, located in Lafayette

County, Wisconsin, has a proud history of successfully educating "our" community's children and youth. As the district responded to new requirements from the state and federal government (for example, "Agenda 2017," which is Wisconsin's plan for every child to graduate college career ready), the main focus was and will remain on providing excellent educational opportunities for all students. As part of raising achievement levels for all students, the district strove to close achievement gaps for students from low-income families and students with disabilities. Raising achievement and closing the achievement gaps are also main focus areas in state report cards, by which all schools in Wisconsin are rated.

The Darlington Community School District serves approximately 810 K–12 students. The four-year-old kindergarten students are housed within three community-based programs. The district has two schools located on one campus: a K–8 elementary/middle school and a 9–12 high school. The elementary/middle school enrollment ranges from 450 to 550 students and the high school enrollment is approximately 225 students. The City of Darlington has about 2,300 residents.

Over the past three years, the district has experienced significant growth in English as Second Language students entering as kindergarteners. The minority population of Lafayette County has increased, with Hispanics and African Americans being the two primary racial/ethnic groups moving into southwestern Wisconsin.

Six Initiatives. Darlington Community School District has become very intentional in adopting research-based educational practices. District leaders have been excited to continue this process, using the most effective curricula, assessments, and interventions to better meet the needs of students while addressing the focus areas in state report cards.

There are six initiatives underway in the district. Each is directly connected to student achievement and pro-social behaviors. Below is a summary of each of the six initiatives:

- Response to Intervention (RTI) is the process of using assessments to identify skills that students have not learned and quickly providing them with interventions to teach those skills.
- Balanced Assessment Systems (BAS) use multiple types of data to inform decisions about student needs. Rather than waiting for the annual state achievement test, we review data more frequently.

- Educator Effectiveness Evaluation (EEE) is the new state model for teacher evaluation involving short, frequent classroom observations, watching for critical teaching strategies.
- Common Core State Standards (CCSS) are higher academic standards that focus teaching on complex skills requiring data analysis, teaming, and higher-order thinking skills.
- Smarter Balanced Assessments (SBA) are the new statewide achievement tests given to all students in grades 3 through 8 beginning in 2015. Results are used for state report cards.
- Positive Behavior Interventions and Supports (PBIS) include the ways to help students learn how to behave in school and maintain high levels of positive behaviors.

Each initiative reflects the direction of the Wisconsin Department of Public Instruction and the influence of Adelman and Taylor's student learning support systems. The development of some initiatives has been ongoing over the past three years, including Common Core State Standards, Response to Intervention, and Balanced Assessment Systems. These initiatives are in various stages of implementation.

Other initiatives are entirely new, having been introduced during the 2013–2014 school year. These initiatives are Educator Effectiveness and Smarter Balanced Assessments. The final initiative, Positive Behavior Interventions and Supports (PBIS), represents a new way of organizing our work on student behaviors using proven strategies. This initiative will be implemented during the 2014–2015 school year.

Five of the six initiatives are required by the state, either through law or administrative rule. The sixth initiative, PBIS, is required in our elementary/middle school due to the fact that this school was identified as a Focus School. Being identified as a Focus School means that the school must focus on, or devote time and effort to, supporting subgroups of students. That is, being identified as a Focus School does not necessarily mean that the school as a whole is performing poorly. PBIS has been shown to raise student achievement while also supporting subgroups of students and improving school climate.

The district curriculum team has created a four-year timeline for implementation of all six initiatives that culminates with the advent of the Smarter Balanced Assessments defined above. By 2015, we expect to have modified many of our practices to better identify and meet the learning needs of our students. In summary, the district is in the midst of significant changes, and looking forward to reporting progress to our community.

FOCUSING ON ONE INITIATIVE: RESPONSE TO INTERVENTION (RTI)

The initiative highlighted in this chapter is Response to Intervention (RTI). This initiative began as a result of the superintendent's dissertation and the influence of Adelman and Taylor's work. The superintendent's vision led to administrative meetings to design the environment, provide staff development, and construct the framework used through the 2012–2013 school year. In late February and early March of 2012, the superintendent set the following ground rules for principals regarding the implementation of Response to Intervention:

- Establish a common district-wide time for RTI so all staff members may be involved.
- Declare that all instructional staff members participate in the interventions.
- Launch and implement RTI programming based upon value-added data and each individual's need for further instruction and strategies.
- Create activities and opportunities for all students to participate in RTI activities no matter their ability level.
- Explain the expected accountability measures from staff on student growth.

The overall expectation of the RTI program was to replace the ways growth was measured by adopting a "value-added" growth model for students. The value-added growth model acknowledges growth regardless of a student's initial benchmark, and essentially provides schools with higher numbers of low-performing students more opportunities for student growth, both in practice and as reflected on the state report card. Value-added growth models can be used to estimate a school's effectiveness by controlling for student characteristics such as prior achievement or poverty.

Schools across the state are struggling to find and implement an RTI time block. By the end of the 2012–2013 school year, principals designed a building schedule that accommodated K–12 students with a twenty-six-minute RTI time block. This schedule change included adding thirteen minutes to the school day and reducing the passing time between secondary classes in each building to three minutes. All teachers participated in implementing the RTI time block during the 2013–2014 school year.

Teachers of high school students have traditionally received their training in one content area and do not always feel equipped to address the needs of students in other content areas. The Darlington high school principal, Doug McArthur, selected the high school English and math certified teachers to identify the students to whom math and reading/language arts interventions would be provided. These teachers used the Measures of Academic Progress (MAP), the Wisconsin Knowledge and Concepts Examination (WKCE), and the American College Testing Suite (ACT) assessments to identify specific students. Staff-supervised time off for coursework was given to students who were not identified to be part of this RTI time block.

Darlington elementary/middle school principal Michelle Savatski charged teachers and staff with addressing reading/language arts curriculum using proven strategies. She selected these content areas due to the overall scores in the reading and language arts segments of the MAP and WKCE assessments. Each teacher and teaching assistant in the building was assigned to a team during the RTI time block prior to the beginning of the school year in order to prepare for this initiative.

As faculty began implementing the RTI time block, it appeared that they struggled with finding resources to address the needs of individual students. Teachers, in many cases, were creating their own resources for individual students' needs, which were very time-intensive tasks. Computer programs were adopted to assist students in math; however, more support was needed in other areas.

Administrators and teachers informed the school board of the need to allocate additional time and support for teachers in order to implement RTI with fidelity. During the first quarter, the school board approved $25,000 to hire substitute teachers, which provided classroom teachers with time to collaborate, research resources needed for RTI, and create lessons and resource materials. This amount was a significant allocation of funds, especially given the relatively small budget of a rural district. Each team in the elementary/middle school was then charged with the task of designing and implementing RTI within the planning time allocated.

RTI at the fifth- and sixth-grade level consists of two six-day rotations. Students are divided into three groups: high/average, low/low average, and enrichment. One rotation consists of fifth-grade high/average students in reading. This group meets with the social studies teacher and band teacher as a large group of twenty-five to thirty students. Meanwhile, the fifth-grade low/low average math students are in math with the math instructor. There are about fifteen students in this math group. A few fifth- and sixth-grade students are in enrichment groups called Battle of the Books with the reading teacher.

The sixth-grade high/average students are with the science and physical education teacher working on math. This, again, is a large group of twenty-five to thirty students. Low/low average reading students are with the reading teacher and an educational assistant for more one-on-one help. As the rotation continues, there is also a sixth-grade enrichment group participating in Battle of the Books with the reading teacher. After six days, fifth- and sixth-grade students switch to a new rotation that involves experiencing each other's grade-level RTI activities. Every few rotations students are rewarded for working to their full potential by participating in other activities. These activities include silent reading in the classroom, studying for upcoming tests, playing in the gym, or other supervised activities.

After the January MAP assessments, groups were reevaluated and some students were reassigned to higher or lower groups. Staff used the MAP assessment scores as well as teacher recommendations for moving students into different groups. All math, reading, and language arts scores were taken into consideration. Based on these data, new groups were formed with a fifth-grade group, a sixth-grade group, and a combined fifth- and sixth-grade group. Substitute teachers taught classes for a half-day each semester while staff met as a team to report regarding what was working and what needed improving to make the RTI time block more effective. This collaboration was extremely beneficial because it occurred during the school day, ensuring all staff was available for discussions about students' progress, the resources needed to move ahead, and any other concerns with the student groupings and implementation.

Materials and Resources. The following paragraphs contain examples of the specific resources and implementations the Darlington Community School District used for their RTI initiative. This information is included to inform boards and superintendents about the level of complexity and resources required to create effective RTI time blocks.

In reading, high/average groups have been using the *A–Z Readers, Scholastic Scope and Storyworks, Time for Kids*, as well as various educational game websites. Because of the large number of students, the social studies and band teachers split the large high/average group in half, and each group participated in the same activity with different materials. With *Scope and Storyworks*, short plays in a reader-theater format were used. As a result, students spent one rotation reading plays and completing vocabulary and comprehension work associated with the play. A second rotation was used to work on presenting the play. The debate component in the *Scope and Storyworks* was also used as a one-rotation activity.

The student-teacher ratio was reduced for the low group because it was led by a teacher and teaching assistant. This group used *A–Z Readers, Soar to Success*, and Readingworks.org. They also subscribed to *Scootpad*. Additionally, they used iPad applications such as *Grammaropolis* and *Wonderous* by Houghton Mifflin. This group also used SpellingCity.com, which is a vocabulary and spelling activity. Progress was monitored as teachers recorded reading comprehension test results, the activity levels that the students completed, and the corresponding improvement or growth evidenced.

Battle of the Books was part of the curriculum for the enrichment group of reading students. There is a need for these students to cultivate self-motivation and engage in more independent learning. Battle of the Books is a six-month activity in which the students choose and read books from a prescribed list and then participate in a statewide competition testing their knowledge and comprehension of the books. At the time of this writing, students were working on student-driven projects that show comprehension of literature and poetry.

Fifth- and sixth-grade RTI high/average math students worked on lessons based on the Common Core State Standards and Smarter Balanced

Assessments. The low/low average students worked on strategies to help close achievement gaps. The work of the low/low average group included basic multiplication and division facts and skills at or below grade level. Through students' MAP assessment results, areas of weakness and work on specific skills were pinpointed. In addition, each student was assigned to *ALEKS*, a research-based, online, adaptive math program. Using the results of the MAP assessment, the *ALEKS* program creates developmentally appropriate math problems that allow students to practice and strengthen their math skills. The *ALEKS* progress-monitoring segment enabled the teacher to track students' success.

The high/average students worked on more challenging problems to advance their skills. These problems were organized and set up by the classroom math teacher. There were three different folder concepts used by the classroom math teacher: (1) On Your Own, (2) With a Partner/Small group, and (3) With the Teacher. Most of the activities were found on mathteachingresources.com and in Smarter Balanced sample test questions. Each student tracked his or her activities on a report sheet inside the folder. This report is stapled to the inside of the student's folder, where it is easy for the classroom math teacher to ascertain which skills the student worked on during the RTI block time. Along with folder activities, the students worked online in Khan Academy. Khan Academy also has a progress-monitoring strand embedded within it.

The folder concept provided monitoring advantages, including the opportunity for teachers to incorporate students' knowledge and understanding into regular classroom activities. Students made connections to skills being taught in class, which in turn provided for discussions about connections with other areas in math.

Although it was a great deal of work preparing the folders, it was worth it. The folder system helped the science and physical education teachers who facilitate the group because the answer keys and strategies were already included on the master copy. The students were also allowed to check their answers from the answer key, and if they had incorrect answers, they were allowed to go back and rework the problems. The opportunity to check answers and rework problems helped develop independent thinking and responsibility.

The Future. As the Darlington Community School District looks forward to the 2014–2015 school year, discussions are underway about the next steps to expand the RTI program throughout the district. Discussions include:

- Adapting job responsibilities with the reading specialist to assist student needs.
- Adjusting the school calendar to allow for staff development, collaboration time, and additional preparation time for staff consistently by offering a 1:30 dismissal time each Friday afternoon in place of our current calendar.
- Involving activities for all students at the high school level.
- Implementing PBIS for the coming year.

ROLES OF THE SCHOOL BOARD AND SUPERINTENDENT IN STUDENT LEARNING SUPPORT SYSTEM INITIATIVES

Based on the experience of the Darlington Community School District in developing a strategic plan for implementing student learning support systems, the following are suggestions for school board members and superintendents:

School Board Members

- Understand and provide resources based on the initiative framework and state requirements in order to properly address the needs of the district.
- Address the issue of time and the allocation thereof for resource mapping: the frequency and duration of time allowed will determine the pace and effectiveness of progress.
- Support the initiatives funding and other necessary resources.
- Request information updates for board meetings to keep the public informed about the initiatives' progress.

Superintendent

- Develop a vision that promotes practices to address individual student growth and college and career readiness skills.

- Continue improving your work as an instructional leader.
- Establish ground rules that support innovative decision making within your district.
- Provide resources and time for staff to plan, develop, and implement strategies.
- Communicate regularly with the board about the needs and progress of the initiatives.
- Expect accountability among staff and administrators.

Role of the Principal

- Implement the district's vision within their schools through the initiatives approved by the school board.
- Monitor staff accountability for initiatives.
- Listen, support, accommodate, and provide resources as needed.
- Allow for flexibility within the school while maintaining the fidelity of the initiative.
- Create the avenue for collaborative problem solving.

Teachers

- Value all students of all ability levels.
- Possess a strong understanding of grade-level and subject-level curriculum.
- Possess knowledge and time to review data a minimum of three times during the school year.
- Allow for flexibility of programming to build ownership and address individual needs of both students and staff.
- Commit to collaboration by grade level and subject area.
- Commit to communication with administrator to address barriers with the process.

Factors to Consider When Developing Programs

- Administrators and board members must listen to and celebrate with all stakeholders the successes and address the weaknesses.

- Administrators must acknowledge that what works within one grade level or group one year may not work within the same grade level or group the following year.
- All staff must allow for flexibility.
- All staff must look for ways to improve and adapt processes to meet the needs of all students.

Additional Recommendations

In summary, it is recommended that superintendents and boards focus on the following practical considerations:

- All stakeholders and constituents need to be aware of the benefits of comprehensive student support systems.
- A plan for student comprehensive support systems should include professional development that addresses time and is monitored for accountability. Key question: What do teachers emphasize during instructional delivery?
- A plan for student comprehensive support systems should include collaboration time that is "vertical or horizontal" by design to include collaboration across grade levels or subject areas as well as collaboration at grade level or subject area.
- A plan for student comprehensive support systems should include time for staff reflection, practice, and implementation.

SUMMARY

Comprehensive student support systems facilitate school improvement planning in three important ways: (1) supporting individual student achievement, (2) preparing students for college and careers beyond achievement test scores, and (3) supporting staff collaboration to improve instruction and delivery.

A culture of school improvement is firmly embedded in the Darlington Community School District using state and local accountability structures. By focusing on the need to provide comprehensive student support systems as part of a larger school improvement effort, board and superintendent dialogue about all of the components of a comprehensive student support system are critical to student success.

RTI as one aspect of the school improvement culture in the Darlington Community School District was the focus of this chapter. The evaluation and inventory of resources in a school district through the resource and management processes defined by Adelman and Taylor (2008) are initial steps to school improvement planning and lend themselves to defining and establishing RTI policies and practices. School improvement planning provides an avenue for all stakeholders to understand the district's resources, the effectiveness of these resources, and student needs that may not be clearly identified and addressed within the curriculum, school, and/or individual's learning plan. Evaluating resources is an important step in moving forward to effective change.

Program evaluation, resource assessment, and providing various tiers of student interventions and support, as demonstrated by the RTI model, are critical components of Adelman and Taylor's comprehensive student support systems. This chapter provided many details of partial implementation of various aspects of Adelman and Taylor's model. School board members and superintendents play a key leadership role in providing structure so that students and staff can benefit from a multilayered approach to assessment and instruction aimed at raising achievement for all students.

ADDITIONAL MATERIALS

The work of Adelman and Taylor at the Center for Mental Health in Schools at UCLA has been prolific, productive, and beneficial to the profession. It is our opinion that Adelman and Taylor are very approachable and responsive professionals. They listen to issues and consider local, state, and national politics when they consult with individuals. Obviously, we have the highest regard for their work and consider them to be a tremendous resource for boards of education and superintendents. For this chapter, we reviewed three of their textbooks and are aware of approximately twenty online National Center at UCLA documents that can assist boards and superintendents.

We highly recommend the following two articles:

A. The abstract for "District Superintendents and School Improvement: Problem of Addressing Barriers to Learning," September 2011, states:

> This report begins with conclusions drawn from a wide range of research, reports, and other sources that convey what superintendents say is driving their work. The focus first is on what they identify as the challenges and frustrations of the job and what they say are factors interfering with student progress. Then, discussion turns to the insufficient way the majority of districts appear to address barriers to learning and teaching, and what some trailblazing superintendents are doing to be more productive in this arena. Finally, implications are outlined for a central office organization that can more effectively enhance equal opportunity for all students to succeed at school and beyond.

B. The 2004 article regarding school boards is entitled "Restructuring Boards of Education to Enhance School Effectiveness in Addressing Barriers to Student Learning." The abstract states:

> The document is meant to encourage school boards to take another critical step in improving schools, specifically by focusing on how the district and each school address barriers to learning and teaching. The discussion explores:
>
> - Why school boards need to increase their focus on addressing barriers to learning and teaching
> - The benefits accrued from doing so
> - Ways to build an enhanced focus on addressing barriers into a school board's committee structure
> - Lessons learned from a major district where the board created a committee dedicated to improving how current resources are expended to address barriers to learning and teaching.

The full report can be downloaded at: http://smhp.psych.ucla.edu/pdf docs/boardrep.pdf.

REFERENCES

Adelman, H. S., and Taylor, L. (2004). *Restructuring boards of education to enhance schools' effectiveness in addressing barriers to student learning.* Los Angeles: Center for Mental Health in Schools, UCLA. http://smhp.psych.ucla.edu.

Adelman, H. S., and Taylor, L. (2006a). *The implementation guide to student learning supports in the classroom and school wide.* Thousand Oaks, CA: Corwin.

Adelman, H. S., and Taylor, L. (2006b). *Resource mapping, and management to address barriers to learning: An intervention for systemic change.* Los Angeles: Center for Mental Health in Schools, UCLA. http://smhp.psych.ucla.edu.

Adelman, H. S., and Taylor, L. (2006c) *The school leader's guide to student learning supports.* Thousand Oaks, CA: Corwin.

Adelman, H. S., and Taylor, L. (2008). *Rebuilding for learning: Addressing barriers to learning and teaching and re-engaging students.* New York: Scholastic.

Adelman, H. S., and Taylor, L. (2011). *District superintendents and the school improvement problem of addressing barriers to learning.* Los Angeles: Center for Mental Health in Schools, UCLA. http://smhp.psych.ucla.edu.

Wellnitz, D. (2008). *Resource mapping and management to address barriers to learning: An intervention for systemic change.* EdD dissertation, Edgewood College, Madison, Wisconsin.

4

ALTERNATIVE COMPENSATION MODELS

Daniel W. Olson and Amy E. Van Deuren

This chapter is intended to provide both boards and superintendents with a detailed overview of alternative compensation plans in the context of today's prevalent single-salary schedule. Included is a history of compensation reforms, a history of teacher pay structures in the United States, a general description of common alternate compensation approaches, specific examples of alternative compensation implementations, and theoretical arguments for and against alternative compensation.

Whether or not your district is considering the implementation of an alternative compensation model, the information in this chapter will help all members of the board/superintendent team understand the background and history of this critical aspect of district leadership. Olson (2014) found that both board members and superintendents felt that they needed to know more about teacher compensation. In addition, he found that many districts that adopt alternate compensation models tend to choose one model as a foundation and then customize it to meet the needs of their districts.

For nearly a century, most teacher compensation plans have been based on a single-salary schedule that rewarded teachers with additional pay for years of teaching experience in a single district and completion of graduate coursework (Kelley and Odden, 1995). The single-salary schedule emerged in the early part of the twentieth century in response to discrimination in the former pay structure, which was essentially a differentiated pay model that compensated high school teachers and men more than elementary school teachers and women. In 2008, approximately 95 percent of public school teachers in the United States were paid using a traditional single-salary schedule (Wisconsin Center for Education Research, 2008).

The strength of teacher unions and the simplicity of the single-salary schedule have contributed to its popularity among teachers as well as its longevity as a viable salary solution in school districts throughout the nation. The system has the added benefit of being "fair" on its face because teacher salaries are public record. While the single-salary schedule has positive aspects that have contributed to its longevity, it creates little or no connection between the performance or productivity of teachers and the compensation they receive. A growing body of research indicates that the current single-salary structure may be ineffective and outdated as it relates to student performance and teacher productivity and motivation (Kelley and Odden, 1995; Odden and Kelley, 2002).

Proponents of education reform have advocated for policies aimed at creating what some believe is a more equitable compensation structure for teachers. Political and market-based pressures are causing school boards to investigate performance-based pay, incentive pay, and other alternative methods of teacher compensation beyond the traditional single-salary schedule. Podgursky and Springer (2006) found that even the government civil service pay system "is more flexible and market-based than those found in most traditional public schools" (p. 3).

While the problems with the single-salary structure have been clearly identified in the research, it is not clear whether alternative compensation plans will fare any better. That being said, many school districts are looking at various alternative compensation models as a way to connect compensation more directly with teacher productivity and student success.

HISTORY OF TEACHER PAY STRUCTURES IN THE UNITED STATES

The history of teacher compensation in the United States can be characterized by slow, gradual changes in structure. Since the 1800s, "there have been only three major changes in the method of teacher pay: an initial rural tradition of paying teachers room and board, a move to a grade-based salary schedule, and finally, the shift to today's single schedule" (Protsik, 1995, p. 1).

Boarding Round System. In the early 1880s, most Americans lived in rural areas and had limited money to provide compensation for teachers. This led to the "boarding round" pay system, which was well suited for the agriculturally based economies of the United States during this time period.

Teacher compensation consisted primarily of room and board provided by the local community. The free room and board provided an incentive for teachers to have good moral character and build strong community ties because they relied on the community for their compensation (Consortium for Policy Research in Education, 2012). This initial tradition of paying teachers room and board with a modest salary was originally negotiated between a teacher and the school board. These early rural teachers were predominantly young women, and classrooms centered on reciting and memorizing content using material like the McGuffey Readers (Odden and Kelley, 1997).

Grade-Based Salary System. In the mid-nineteenth century, the boarding round system was replaced by a grade-based salary system. In the grade-based salary system, teachers were paid based on their years of experience, gender, race, and the grade level taught (Protsik, 1995). This system paid elementary teachers less than secondary teachers, and women and minority teachers less than nonminority males (Kelley and Odden, 1995). This inequity in teacher pay led, in part, to the creation of the single-salary schedule (Odden and Kelley, 2002).

Single-Salary Schedule. The first single-salary systems were implemented in Denver and Des Moines in 1921 (Gratz, 2005). The purpose was to pay teachers on the same scale, regardless of gender, race, or grade level taught. Under the single-salary plan, all teachers were paid equally based on their years of experience and degrees earned. Teachers who had the same amount of experience and education were paid the same; no differentiation relative to teacher success in the classroom was made. The single-salary system accelerated in use by districts throughout the country around the time of World War II. By 1950, 97 percent of all schools had adopted the single-salary schedule (Protsik, 1995).

The single-salary schedule is the most common pay system for teachers in the United States because it is equitable for teachers, objective, and easy to administer (Odden and Kelley, 2002). All teachers had an equal chance of earning a pay raise under the same rules of experience and personal education level. A greater number of teachers were encouraged, as a result, to earn advanced education degrees beyond their current level. Murray and Brown (2003) suggested that schools and teachers accepted the single-salary schedule because it was easier to understand; it was easier to budget for anticipated salary increases, and it was easier to discuss in collective bargaining.

Odden and Kelley (2002) described separate studies that found many of the credits used as a basis for salary increases were only loosely, if at all, connected to teaching responsibilities or to emerging notions of challenging subject matter instruction. Brown and Heywood (2002) argued that schools foster an undesirable culture of mediocrity by treating every teacher the same. Protsik (1995) found that teachers often lack sufficient incentive to expand their own skills necessary to work with high standards curriculum or to work in site-based managed schools.

A new conventional wisdom among education reformers is emerging, suggesting that the single-salary system is outmoded. The traditional system, reformers argue, fails to attract the best college graduates into teaching and provides practicing teachers no incentives to produce results. Low beginning salaries for teachers are additionally unattractive to high-performing teachers limited in salary advancement by the steps and lanes of the single-salary schedule. Despite the imperfections of the single-salary schedule, its significant advantages of familiarity, predictability, and ease of administration have made it resistant to change (Odden and Kelley, 2002).

Boards and superintendents have many new initiatives that could be tied to compensation if they chose to do so. Odden and Kelley (2002) cite state standards, student assessments, teacher evaluation, technology, group-based performance, and individual knowledge and skills as the foundations for the new environment in public education. There's an old saying that "there's nothing new in education," and the same could be said of the initiatives listed above; however, the convergence of all of these initiatives in today's political, social, and economic climate create a unique opportunity to rethink teacher compensation.

MODELS OF ALTERNATIVE COMPENSATION

Many past attempts to link pay to performance were quickly abandoned by school districts, raising questions about the effectiveness of these systems (Odden and Kelley, 1997). Firestone (1994) found that previous attempts to "reform the single-salary schedule have usually left it intact but added an individual incentive component such as merit pay or career ladders" (p. 552). The following is an overview of the most common alternate compensation models in use in the United States. These systems typically use a base salary approach, which is derived from the single-salary schedule or some version thereof.

Merit Pay. Merit pay has existed for over a hundred years in the United States, ever since the establishment of the first plan in Newton, Massachusetts, in 1908 (Protsik, 1995). But the real impetus for merit pay began in the 1960s in the aftermath of Sputnik. According to Cohen and Murnane (1985), "one study reported that the chief local reasons for abandoning merit pay included teachers' discontent with merit ratings and the difficulties of devising a scientifically defensible measure of teacherly merit" (p. 6).

In the 1980s, following the publication of *A Nation at Risk* (1983), merit pay systems once again flourished briefly (Gratz, 2005). Inman (1985) cited low teacher salaries as the reason for "the underlying problems associated with the poor quality of public education" (p. 41). Inman traced the political interest in merit pay in the 1980s to former Tennessee Governor (and later U.S. Secretary of Education) Lamar Alexander's career ladder proposal but noted that Florida was actually the first to enact a "master teacher law."

Wilms and Chapleau (1999) argued that tying student test scores to teacher or administrator pay not only fails to improve student achievement, but also is destructive. "Shifting the focus of education from the student to the pocketbook erodes teachers' professional judgment and demeans the process of education" (p. 48). Kelley and Odden (1995) found merit pay programs promoted competition among teachers and prevented them from collaborating.

Kohn (2003) offered several reasons why merit pay systems have been largely unsuccessful. Merit pay may feel manipulative and patronizing to teachers because those in control and with power are the ones to set goals, establish criteria, and assess results. The accountability is shifted to the teachers, who have little input about the elements of the system. Additionally, merit pay programs can create high-stakes cheating, or gaming, which encourages teachers to teach to the test without improving student learning. Kohn argued alternatively that "teachers should be paid well, freed from misguided mandates, treated with respect, and provided with the support they need to help their students become increasingly proficient and enthusiastic learners" (p. 44).

McCollum (2001) found that merit pay programs failed, and most were discontinued within six years for several reasons, including the following: (a) supporting legislators leaving office, (b) programs implemented unfairly, (c) teachers' unions refusal to endorse them, (d) low teacher morale created by competition for limited dollars, and (e) costly programs that were difficult to administer.

Dickson (1990) cited the primary reason for the failure of merit pay programs was teacher dissatisfaction with evaluation procedures. "Districts found it difficult to determine who actually deserved extra pay, ratings were not seen as accurate, data was insufficient to support evaluations and instruments and evaluations were found to be subjective and unreliable" (p. 3). Feldman (2000) found that merit pay plans failed because the plans often lacked objective criteria. More than one researcher attributed the failure of merit pay systems directly to resistance from teachers and teacher unions (Ballou, 2001; Odden and Kelley, 2002).

Although there are several reasons that merit pay failed, boards and superintendents should be aware that it has been successful as well under certain conditions. Murnane and Cohen (1986) found that school districts with merit pay plans lasting a number of years had several common characteristics: (a) teacher morale was high; (b) merit pay was not promoted as a means to punish ineffective teachers; (c) housing costs were high (an indication of the community's affluence); (d) there was support for public schools; (e) teacher salaries on the uniform salary schedule were high prior to the introduction of merit pay; and (f) the existing evaluation policies functioned well.

Career Ladders. In the later 1980s, career ladder programs were developed and implemented by several states (Odden and Kelley, 2002). Career ladder programs link teacher pay to career-level advancement within the profession. Teachers in a career ladder program receive a salary increase as they climb up from one rung of the ladder to the next. Teachers on higher rungs generally have more responsibilities such as curriculum development and mentoring (Protsik, 1995).

Kelley and Odden (1995) distinguished career ladders from merit pay by describing a career ladder as an opportunity to "alter the flat career structure of teaching" by providing opportunities beyond the regular classroom (p. 1). Odden and Kelley (2002) described the career ladders of the 1980s as systems that were designed to identify the best teachers and give them "leadership positions, such as curriculum or professional development" while keeping them in the classroom (p. 37).

Though less controversial than merit pay, career ladder programs were also considered to be unsuccessful in reforming teacher compensation (Conley and Odden, 1994). Many career ladder programs failed because teachers were often not involved in the design of the plans, and funding was often cut shortly after inception. Teacher union opposition was also cited as a cause of career ladder failure (Odden and Kelley, 2002).

Knowledge and Skill-Based Pay Systems. Stronge, Gareis, and Little (2006) described knowledge and skill-based pay systems as competency pay designed to reward teachers on the basis of professional growth. They identified three categories of "skill blocks" to determine teacher competencies: (a) "depth skills" as grade-level or content-area skills, (b) "breadth skills" as lateral skills or those skills outside of one's current "depth," and (c) "vertical skills" as the "development of leadership and management competencies" (p. 14).

Milanowski (2002) suggested that knowledge and skill-based pay systems could be used to motivate teachers to acquire better pedagogical skills. However, simply paying bonuses to encourage teachers to acquire such skills would not be sufficient to improve instruction. He determined that teachers must be paid based upon the student achievement that results from teachers' newly acquired pedagogical skills.

Firestone (1994) found that knowledge and skill-based pay systems created significant additional costs to school districts in the form of expenditures for professional development and "measurement work." He stated that in the private sector, increased costs for similar pay systems could be offset by increased profits as a natural result of higher productivity.

Collective Incentives. Stronge, Gareis, and Little (2006) defined collective incentives as "school-based incentive awards" awarded to teachers based on group increases in student achievement at the school, grade, or department level (p. 12). Teachers may receive school-based performance awards in the form of individual bonuses, or money may be placed in the school budget to be used for professional development activities. Firestone (1994) noted that collective incentives are generally based on a limited number of broad "outcomes . . . relevant to all of the teachers in a school" (p. 561).

Collective incentives assume the entire faculty, administration, support staff, and student body must work together to produce achievement results. Collective incentives can also provide an important symbolic focus on outcomes while avoiding divisive aspects of performance incentives. Collective initiatives can also work well if individual roles are clearly identified and clear accountability mechanisms are in place.

Critics of collective incentive plans point out that not all teachers in the group have an equal impact on improving student achievement. Some teachers will do their best to work together to improve student outcomes while others will not work as hard but still benefit from the group achievement. Solmon and Podgursky (2000) identified this as the "free rider effect," whereby some teachers may not put forth as much effort believing the others in the group will work harder to achieve the desired outcomes (p. 2).

Market-Based Pay. Market-based pay generally refers to providing bonuses or other compensation to attract teachers in hard-to-fill areas such as mathematics, science, technology, and special education (Odden and Wallace, 2004). Prince (2003) found that a number of approaches to compensating teachers for hard-to-staff positions existed. Compensation could be in the forms of signing bonuses, targeted salary increases, housing incentives, tuition assistance, or even tax incentives.

Two ways that market-based pay systems are used include local or state-issued incentives to teach in areas experiencing teacher shortages and loan forgiveness programs. Two examples of these market-based pay systems that boards and superintendents might want to consider are presented below.

The Teachers of Tomorrow Program was established in New York State in 2000 to assist school districts in the recruitment, retention, and certification activities necessary to increase the supply of qualified teachers in school districts experiencing teacher shortages. Teachers could receive incentives of $15,000 a year or more, depending on the school district and their levels of certification. The U.S. Department of Education supports two types of loan forgiveness programs to encourage individuals to enter and continue in the teaching profession. The Teacher Loan Forgiveness Program allows up to $17,500 of forgiveness on certain federal student loans for teachers of science, mathematics, and special education, while the Teacher Cancellation Program allows for cancellation of up to 100 percent of Federal Perkins Loans for teachers of federally designated shortage areas (U.S. Department of Education, 2012).

RECENTLY IMPLEMENTED ALTERNATIVE COMPENSATION PROGRAMS: SPECIFIC EXAMPLES

While merit pay and career ladders have comprised the majority of alternative compensation models, new performance-based programs have gained substantial popularity in the last decade. The various models take into consideration different elements when developing a pay structure to fit the unique needs of the district being served.

Numerous programs have emerged at the national, state, and district levels in which teachers' pay is linked to some aspects of their performance. According to Podgursky and Springer (2006), most recent performance pay programs maintain the steps and lanes pay schedule and offer teachers the opportunity to earn additional onetime bonuses conditioned on annual performance measures.

Department of Education's Teacher Incentive Fund (TIF). In 2006, the U.S. Congress appropriated $99 million per year for five years for the Teacher Incentive Fund (TIF) (Springer, 2009). This grant process was developed as a companion to NCLB and was aimed at encouraging experimentation with performance pay (Gratz, 2009a). These funds were available to school districts, charter schools, and states on a competitive basis to fund both principal and teacher pay-for-performance programs. The goals of TIF included the following:

- Improving student achievement by increasing teacher and principal effectiveness;

- Reform teacher and principal compensation systems so that teachers and principals are rewarded for increases in student achievement;
- Increase the number of effective teachers teaching poor, minority, and disadvantaged students in hard-to-staff subjects; and
- Create a performance-based compensation system. (Gratz, 2009a, p. 238)

The U.S. Department of Education awarded ten grants in the fall of 2006, and another eighteen in 2007 (Gratz, 2009a). According to the Center for Educator Compensation Reform (2012), there are currently ninety-five TIF grantees in various-sized school districts.

ASPIRE in Houston, Texas. The Houston Independent School District first implemented a wide-ranging performance pay program in 2005 and 2006. The program, now called Accelerating Student Progress: Increasing Results and Expectations (ASPIRE), focuses on student achievement demonstrated on standardized tests. The four primary components of the plan are: (1) Value-Added Campus Improvement, (2) Teacher Progress, (3) Campus Improvement Awards, and (4) Campus Achievement Awards (Johnson and Papay, 2009).

The ASPIRE program is one of the largest and most successful performance pay plans in the nation (Mellon, 2010). By 2010, the program had provided over $113 million in performance pay bonuses (Johnson and Papay, 2009). Bonuses were given to teachers whose students made the biggest gains academically and ranged from $25 to nearly $25,000 (Mellon, 2010). This program resulted in almost 90 percent of the eligible employees earning a bonus. Bonuses were paid to schools based on their test scores, as well as to individual teachers based on their students' scores (Johnson and Papay, 2009). The school board has used this pay system as a method to attract and retain the best teachers (Mellon, 2010).

Denver Public Schools' Professional Compensation System for Teachers (ProComp). The Denver Professional Compensation (ProComp) system is perhaps the most well-known reform model of teacher pay. ProComp is "a comprehensive amalgam of successful teaching and service to the school community" (Gratz, 2009a, p. 86). ProComp does not solely base the extra compensation on student test scores. Teachers can earn additional funds for working in hard-to-staff schools, teaching in high-needs areas, and attending professional development workshops

(Ramirez, 2010/2011). "While ProComp is widely touted as a pay-for performance plan, in fact it is but one component of a more comprehensive pay reform" (Springer, 2009, p. 29).

The four components of ProComp (2012) are as follows:

- *Knowledge and Skills*. Teachers will earn compensation for acquiring and demonstrating knowledge and skills by completing annual professional development units, through earning additional graduate degrees and national certificates, and may be reimbursed up to $1,000 annually, $4,000 lifetime for tuition and repayment of student loans.
- *Professional Evaluation*. Teachers were recognized for their classroom skill by receiving salary increases every three years for satisfactory evaluations.
- *Student Growth*. Teachers were rewarded for the academic growth of their students. They can earn compensation for meeting annual objectives, for exceeding the Colorado Student Assessment Program growth goals, and for working in a school judged distinguished based on academic gains and other factors.
- *Market Incentives*. Bonuses can assist the district and schools in meeting specific needs. Teachers in hard-to-serve schools, those faced with academic challenges, can earn annual bonuses. Bonuses were available to those filling hard-to-staff positions, assignments which historically have shortages of qualified applicants. (para. 3–6)

Denver public school teachers attribute the success of ProComp to the increased district and school focus on student achievement, individual goal setting, and the professional development received in the areas of setting and measuring goals. In addition, teachers attributed success to motivation factors other than incentive pay because they were actively involved in the process, and their expertise was acknowledged and utilized (Gratz, 2009a).

Minnesota's Q-Comp. In 2005, Minnesota adopted Quality Compensation for Teachers or Q-Comp. The Q-Comp program is a statewide voluntary performance pay program that rewards participating school districts with increased funding up to $260 per student. To participate in Q-Comp, the district must design and implement a plan that provides teacher bonuses that link to student performance and subjective performance evaluations.

Q-Comp provides flexibility in how districts design their performance pay plans, but each district is required to align at least 60 percent of teacher bonuses to measures of student academic achievement and progress. The average Q-Comp plan offers teachers the opportunity to earn over $2,000 in annual bonuses if the teacher meets specific performance targets (Sojourner, West, and Mykerezi, 2011). Q-Comp districts typically award performance bonuses based on subjective performance evaluations, the teacher's own students' performance, and school-wide student performance measures. Current Q-Comp plans typically attach the highest bonus awards to subjective performance evaluations.

Milken Family Foundation's Teacher Advancement Program (TAP). The Teacher Advancement Program (TAP) was developed in the late 1990s by the Milken Family Foundation (MFF) to improve individual schools by raising teacher quality. The program includes a comprehensive strategy with the following four key principles: (1) multiple career paths, (2) market-driven compensation, (3) performance-based accountability, and (4) expanding the supply of highly qualified teachers (Milken, 2000). TAP has been implemented in more than two hundred schools in thirteen states around the country and is overseen by the National Institute for Excellence in Teaching (NIET), an organization started by MFF (Glazerman and Seifullah, 2012).

Under the TAP model, teachers can earn extra pay by increasing responsibilities through promotion (to mentor teacher or master teacher), and they are eligible for annual performance bonuses based on a combination of their contribution to student achievement (known as "value-added") and observed performance in the classroom. The idea behind the program is that giving teachers performance incentives, along with tools to track their performance and improve instruction, will help schools attract and retain talented teachers and help all teachers raise student achievement (Solmon and Podgursky, 2000; Glazerman and Seifullah, 2012).

SUMMARY

While numerous alternative systems of paying teachers have been tried over the years, the traditional single-salary schedule has remained the most prevalent for several reasons. The single-salary schedule is easy to administer; it is objective; it encourages teachers to seek advanced degrees; and it eliminated the inequities of paying women less than men, minorities less than nonminorities, and elementary teachers less than secondary teachers.

While there is general agreement that the single-salary schedule may not be the most effective way to pay teachers, there is not agreement on what alternative compensation models should be used. However, there are several good reasons for states and local school districts to consider teacher compensation reform. Proposals to change the way teachers are paid are more popular than ever in both political and policymaker conversations, and recent national commissions on teaching have highlighted teacher compensation reform efforts.

More school districts and states are experimenting with new compensation models than ever before. Finally, the TIF program being operated by the U.S. Department of Education as well as private foundations such as MFF can potentially provide funding to implement alternative compensation systems.

Teacher salaries and benefits typically comprise over 80 percent of a district's budget. The ways this compensation is allocated is an important consideration for boards and superintendents. Teacher compensation is an issue throughout the United States in terms of student achievement and teacher satisfaction and effectiveness. A high-performing board/superintendent team concerned about making decisions that positively impact student achievement will want to be very well informed about their district's own compensation plan and other possible compensation models that may move the district toward achieving the goals in the long-range plan, mission, and vision.

REFERENCES

Ballou, D. (2001). Pay for performance in public and private schools. *Economics of Education Review* 20(1), 51–61.

Brandt, R. M. (1990). *A close up look: Third party evaluation of program components*. Retrieved from ERIC Database (ED324288).

Brown, M., and Heywood, J. S. (2002). Paying for performance: Setting the stage. In M. Brown and J. S. Heywood (Eds.), *Paying for performance: An international comparison* (pp. 3–15). Armonk, NY: M. E. Sharpe.

Center for Educator Compensation Reform. (2012). Retrieved from http://www.cecr.ed.gov.

Chang, R. G. L. (1999). *Current teachers' compensation systems and their perceived effects on motivation.* PhD dissertation, University of Southern California. Available from ProQuest Dissertations and Theses database (UMI No. 3110946).

Cohen, D. K., and Murnane, R. J. (1985). The merits of merit pay. *Public Interest 80*(3), 3–31.

Conley, S., and Odden, A. (1994). *Linking teacher compensation to teacher career development.* Retrieved from ERIC Database (ED380895).

Consortium for Policy Research in Education. (2012). Retrieved from http://www.cpre.org.

Dickson, L. (1990). *Student achievement and career ladder status.* Retrieved from ERIC Database (ED324775).

Feldman, S. (2000). True merit pay. *National Journal 32*(11), 757–57.

Firestone, W. A. (1991, October). Merit pay and job enlargement as reforms: Incentives, implementation, and teacher response. *Educational Evaluation and Policy Analysis 13*(3), 269–88.

Firestone, W. A. (1994). Redesigning teacher salary systems for educational reform. *American Educational Research Journal 31*(3), 549–74.

French, R. L. (1985). Career ladder plans. In P. R. Burden (Ed.), *Establishing career ladders in teaching* (pp. 18–33). Springfield, IL: Charles C. Scott.

Glazerman, S., and Seifullah, A. (2012). *An evaluation of the Chicago teacher advancement program (Chicago TAP) after four years. Final report.* Mathematica Policy Research, Inc. Retrieved from ERIC Database (ED530098).

Gratz, D. B. (2005). Lessons from Denver: The pay for performance pilot. *Phi Delta Kappan 86*(8), 569–81.

Gratz, D. B. (2009a). *The perils and promise of performance pay: Making education compensation work.* Lanham, MD: Rowman & Littlefield Education.

Gratz, D. B. (2009b, November). The problem with performance pay. *Educational Leadership 67*(3), 76–79.

Harris, D. C. (2007). *The promises and pitfalls of alternative teacher compensation approaches.* East Lansing, MI: The Great Lakes Center for Education Research & Practice. Retrieved from http://www.greatlakescenter.org.

Hassel, B. C. (2002). *Better pay for better teaching: Making teaching compensation pay off in the age of accountability.* Washington, DC: Progressive Policy Institute 21st Century Schools Project.

Hirsch, E. (2006). *Recruiting and retaining teachers in Alabama: Educators on what it will take to staff all classrooms with quality teachers.* Chapel Hill, NC: Southeast Center for Teaching Quality.

Inman, D. (1985). The rhetoric and reality of merit pay: Why are they different? In H. C. Johnson (Ed.), *Merit, money and teachers' careers* (pp. 41–56). Lanham, MD: University Press of America, Inc.

Johnson, S. M., and Papay, J. P. (2009). *Redesigning teacher pay: A system for the next generation of educators*. Washington, DC: Economic Policy Institute.

Johnson, S. M., and Papay, J. P. (2010, May). Merit pay for a new generation. *Educational Leadership* 67(8), 48–52.

Kelley, C., Heneman III, H., and Milanowski, A. (2002). Teacher motivation and school-based performance awards. *Education Administration Quarterly* 38(3), 372–401. DOI: 10.1177/0013161X02383004.

Kelley, C., and Odden, A (1995). *Reinventing teacher compensation systems. CPRE Finance Briefs*. Retrieved from ERIC Database (ED387910).

Kohn, A. (2003, September 17). The folly of merit pay. *Education Week*. Retrieved from http://www.edweek.org.

McCollum, S. (2001, February). How merit pay improves education. *Educational Leadership* 58(5), 21–24.

Mellon, E. (2010, January 27). HISD to pay out more than $40 million in bonuses. *Houston Chronicle*. Retrieved from http://www.chron.com.

Milanowski, A. (2002). *The varieties of knowledge and skill-based pay design: A comparison of seven new pay systems for K–12 teachers*. Retrieved from ERIC Database (ED477655).

Milken, L. (2000). *Teaching as the opportunity: The teacher advancement program*. Retrieved from ERIC Database (ED456116).

Murnane, R. J., and Cohen, D. K. (1986). Merit pay and the evaluation problem: Why most merit pay plans fail and few survive. *Harvard Educational Review* 56(1), 1–17.

Murray, J. E., and Brown, K. (2003). *Paying teachers for their worth: Policies on teacher compensation at the school district and regional levels*. Retrieved from ERIC Database (ED482348).

National Commission on Excellence in Education. (1983). *A nation at risk: The imperative for educational reform*. Washington, DC: U.S. Department of Education.

No Child Left Behind (NCLB) Act of 2001, Pub. L. No. 107-110, § 115, Stat. 1425. (2002). Retrieved from http://www2.ed.gov/legislation/esea02/107-110.pdf.

Odden, A. (2000). New and better forms of teacher compensation are possible. *Phi Delta Kappan* 81(5), 361–66.

Odden, A., and Kelley, C. (1997). *Paying teachers for what they know and do: New and smarter compensation strategies to improve schools*. Thousand Oaks, CA: Corwin Press.

Odden, A., and Kelley, C. (2002). *Paying teachers for what they know and do: New and smarter compensation strategies to improve schools* (2nd ed.). Thousand Oaks, CA: Corwin Press.

Odden, A., and Wallace, M. (2004, October). Experimenting with teacher compensation. *School Administrator 61*(9), 24–28.

Olson, Dan. (2014). *Examination of Wisconsin school district superintendent perceptions regarding alternative teacher compensation systems.* EdD dissertation, Edgewood College, Madison, Wisconsin.

Podgursky, M. J., and Springer, M. G. (2006). Teacher performance pay: A review. Working Paper 2006-01. Nashville, TN: National Center on Performance Incentives at Vanderbilt University.

Prince, C. D. (2003). *Higher pay in hard-to-staff schools.* Lanham, MD: University Press of America, Inc.

ProComp. (2012). Retrieved from http://denverprocomp.dpsk12.org.

Protsik, J. (1995). *History of teacher pay and incentive reforms.* Madison, WI: Consortium for Policy Research in Education.

Ramirez, A. (2010/2011, December/January). Merit pay misfires. *Educational Leadership 68*(4), 55–58.

Sojourner, A., West, K., and Mykerezi, E. (2011). *When does teacher incentive pay raise student achievement? Evidence from Minnesota's Q-comp program.* Retrieved from ERIC Database (ED528841).

Solmon, L. C., and Podgursky, M. (2000). *The pros and cons of performance-based compensation.* Retrieved from ERIC Database (ED445393).

Springer, M. G. (2009). *Performance incentives: Their growing impact on American K–12 education.* Washington, DC: Brookings Institution Press.

Springer, M. G., Ballou, D., Hamilton, L., Le, V., Lockwood, J. R., McCaffrey, D., Pepper, M., and Stecher, B. (2010). *Teacher pay for performance: Experimental evidence from the project on incentives in teaching.* Nashville, TN: National Center on Performance Incentives at Vanderbilt University.

Stronge, J. H., Gareis, C., and Little, C. (2006). *Teacher pay and teacher quality: Attracting, developing, and retaining the best teachers.* Thousand Oaks, CA: Corwin Press.

Taylor, L., Springer, M., and Ehlert, M. (2008). Characteristics and determinants of teacher-designed pay for performance plans: Evidence from Texas' Governor's Educator Excellence Grant (GEEG) program. Working Paper 2008-26. Nashville, TN: National Center on Performance Incentives at Vanderbilt University.

Taylor, L., Springer, M., and Ehlert, M. (2009). Teacher-designed performance pay in Texas. In M. G. Springer (Ed.), *Performance incentives: Their growing impact on American K–12 education* (pp. 191–223). Washington, DC: Brookings Institution Press.

U.S. Department of Education. (2012). *Federal student aid: Teacher loan forgiveness.* Retrieved from http://studentaid.ed.gov/repay-loans/forgiveness-cancellation/charts/teacher.

Wilms, W. W., and Chapleau, R. R. (1999, November). The illusion of paying teachers for student performance. *Education Week 19*(10), 34–48.

Wisconsin Center for Education Research. (2008). *Approaches to alternative teachers compensation: Promises and pitfalls.* Retrieved from http://www.wcer.wisc.edu.

Yuan, K., Le, V., McCaffrey, D. F., Marsh, J. A., Hamilton, L. S., Stecher, B. M., and Springer, M. G. (2013). Incentive pay programs do not affect teacher motivation or reported practices: Results from three randomized studies. *Educational Evaluation and Policy Analysis 35*(1), 3.

5

WHAT BOARDS AND SUPERINTENDENTS SHOULD KNOW ABOUT THE IMPORTANCE OF TEACHERS

Raymond J. Golarz

There is clear agreement that teachers are the critical catalyst for student learning and achievement. The profession of teaching has never received the scrutiny and attention it does today. As political parties and the citizenry argue and debate the worth and direction of public education, millions of teachers go forth each day in our nation's classrooms and successfully attend to the needs of our students.

Board members and superintendents must be well versed in the issues confronting teachers. The following chapter by Dr. Ray Golarz focuses on the emotional component of teaching, including the mission of teaching as a "calling" and the need for all of us to acknowledge this noble profession. Of all the chapters in this book, this chapter goes to the heart of the human interaction called teaching. Dr. Golarz and Marion Golarz expand on these themes in their book *The Problem Isn't Teachers* (2012), which provides stories and essays that tell the truth about the real plight of American education.

BY THEIR FRUITS YE SHALL KNOW THEM

Some years ago, I was sitting at my desk in a primary school classroom contemplating something that had me confused. I recall that my teacher, sensing my uneasiness, walked over to my desk. She then said, "Raymond, you seem bewildered."

I answered, "Yes, I am. I'm all confused."

We then talked awhile of my confusion.

Finally, she said, "Raymond, as you live your life and information comes to you that confuses you, always ask yourself where did the information come from? Did it come from people you know to be honest, moral, and usually well informed? If yes, then you can be fairly sure that the information is true. If, on the other hand, the information comes from people who have a history of dishonesty and deceit and are known to be self-serving, then the information is likely to be a lie. Raymond, for a standard of judgment to use in life regarding what you hear or are told always remember, *'By their fruits ye shall know them.'*"

After leaving that early childhood classroom and ultimately completing my schooling, I myself became a teacher. It was a way of life that captured my heart and still holds me close. It has now been many years since I have, in some form or another, been a member of this profession. And of late, I have been pained by the stones thrown against our educational walls challenging even the very fundamental importance of teachers. I sense and hear so much resentment directed toward the profession. There are now moments when I feel as I did sitting in that primary school classroom chair. I am confused. Is what I'm hearing true? Have we somehow let down a nation? Have we let down the nation to whom we pledged our allegiance each morning with our students, hands over hearts? Was our lifelong gift and the gifts of those who came after us and now teach in our classrooms for naught?

I find myself, in my dark alone moments, looking for guidance. I look for my teacher from so long ago, for I am confused and I can't make it go away.

"Raymond."

"Yes."

"Raymond."

"Yes, I'm here."

"Raymond. Have you forgotten? What did I tell you?"

"You said to me so long ago. 'From where does the information come, that causes your confusion?'"

"And, from where does it come?"

"It comes from a multitude of places. It comes from many who hold political office. It also comes from the very, very rich and the lobbyists they employ to promote changes in legislation and policies to further their own ends. It comes, in addition, from many chambers of commerce and huge banks and financial institutions declared too big to be allowed to fail. It comes also from media sources owned by these institutions. It comes from so many places."

"Raymond. What do you know of the history of information that comes from these places? What have they told you in the past? What have they done in the past? What have been their actions?"

"In the last thirty years they have successfully shifted over half of the entire wealth of the United States to the top 1 percent and in so doing crushed the middle class and laid waste to the poorest of our country; leaving there a devastating loss of resources and inescapable poverty. The millions of the children of the poor are now in a condition of hopelessness."

"So Raymond, what can you, using the wisdom I taught to you so long ago now, say of them?"

"They bear bad fruit."

"So why do you listen to them?"

"I get confused. They sound so believable."

"Raymond, let's end this issue in your mind once and for all. Let us end the confusion. I want you to look around and tell me what you actually see. What you see is the state of these average current fellow Americans that surround you. What are they like? What do you hear about them from people whom you know to be honest, moral, and well-informed? Once and for all let's put an end to your confusion. Tell me about *them*."

"Well . . . with few exceptions they seem to be hardworking. I understand that as employees, they are known to have just about the highest productivity level of any workers throughout the world."

"And Raymond, forgive my interruption, from where do you believe that they learned this strong work ethic?"

"From their homes, churches, and schools."

"Go on."

"They seem to be so generous—particularly the working class and the poor. It has often been noted that if you come to them with nothing they will share the little that they have. I've heard it called their 'Amazing Grace.'"

"And Raymond, again from where does this strength of character come?"

"I believe again from their homes, churches, and schools."

"Continue."

"Okay. I reviewed rather recently the Harvard Kennedy School's Global Challenge Report of 2011 comparing the individual states' standings in math and reading with international scores. I find that if you correct and compensate for American poverty in our large- and medium-sized cities and for the poverty of the massive numbers of rural poor then we compare quite favorably with even the wealthiest of international populations. *The problems of our nation are not bad public schools, nor poorly performing teachers."*

"Keep going."

"This last winter I was watching a Sunday evening *60 Minutes* program. The program was reporting on the continuing national disaster of the hundreds of thousands of 'underwater' home ownerships—the condition where existing mortgages are greater than the apprised home value. The program reported that if all homeowners currently suffering this condition 'walked away,' thus giving up their homes, the American economy *would collapse*. They concluded their report with interviews of such homeowners. The remarks of those interviewed had one common theme. And I paraphrase: 'It would be immoral for me to walk away. This is a debt I owe and I must see it through.' The program hosts advised that this was the common and consistent theme that they were hearing in every part of our country."

"Raymond, if I may, where do you think this strong sense of morality comes from in so many of these young and middle-aged Americans?"

"From the teachings in their homes, churches, and schools."

"Continue, please."

"One of my older sons is a lieutenant colonel in the United States Army. He advises me that our military has a complement of fourteen battle carrier groups and, in addition, our army is by far the most technically astute and well-trained of any army in the world. Our recruits come from American public high schools, technical schools, and colleges."

"Coming from where?"

"American public high schools, technical schools, and colleges."

"And from where do the workmen, electricians, welders, and steelmakers who build all of the countless ships come from?"

"Again, they come from our American high schools, technical schools, and colleges."

"Continue please."

"My daughter's husband is a young engineer working for a firm in Illinois. He grew up on a farm. Some months ago, in his plant, a very complex piece of equipment broke down. The downtime was costing the company thousands of dollars a day. They flew in a team from Japan to correct the malfunction. After a week of twelve-hour days the team acknowledged defeat. In desperation, they turned to my son-in-law, the young engineer. He went to Walmart, then Radio Shack—places he had often frequented while growing up on the farm. Places he had gone to get makeshift parts to repair various pieces of farm equipment. He spent $3.49 that afternoon and by day's end he had repaired the $9,000,000 dollar piece of equipment. It ran fine after that."

I continued with another story.

"From my father I was told of how a handful of American soldiers during World War II, overwhelmed by superior numbers and better equipment, repaired their own American tanks on the battlefield to win the Battle of the Bulge."

"And Raymond what is this called, this quality possessed by your son-in-law and young soldiers serving our country on battlefields?"

"It's called American ingenuity."

"And where does it come from?"

"It comes from American homes and garages and farms and classrooms."

"Go ahead, continue."

"My youngest son needed to enroll early for his university advanced chemistry course and microbiology course last week. There are apparently so many foreign students in our country from China, India, Korea, and Japan wanting these same courses that the courses fill up quickly."

"And your son's preparation for these courses came from . . . ?"

"His home, his American high school, and college work."

"Raymond, I understand that our nation consistently wins more medals at international sporting events, such as the Olympics, than any nation on the earth and that throughout the entire country there are middle schools, high schools, and colleges that have competitive sports for men, women, and the handicapped. Can you tell me, Raymond, from which profession in America do those who guide, train, and coach all of these young people come from?"

"They are teachers. They come from the ranks of our American teachers."

"Raymond, have you listened now to the honest, moral, and informed?"

"Yes, I have."

"And what do you now conclude? What do you now know?"

"The profession of American teachers has always and continues to bear good fruit."

"I'm leaving you now, Raymond. You have remembered the lesson, so I need not stay. Tell others what you have seen and heard here today. Tell the school board member who may be confused. Remind the superintendent who may be overwhelmed. Tell the young and doubting teacher. But most of all, tell the many Americans young or old, who for whatever reasons find themselves confused. Remind all of them always how to judge the truth of what they hear with this key phrase: *By their fruits ye shall know them.* Tell them this and tell them to remember. Tell them to remember always."

6

TECHNOLOGY IN SCHOOLS

The Role of Boards and Superintendents

Valerie Schmitz, Amy E. Van Deuren, and Thomas F. Evert

School board members and superintendents deal with a wide range of significant issues, including accountability, state standards, and closing achievement gaps. Technology is a critical tool to help educators provide content and deliver instruction to meet goals tied to these significant issues.

As technology in PK–12 public schools becomes the norm, it is worth looking back at and identifying various historical periods to better understand the changes that have occurred regarding the ways students acquire and use information and knowledge. Smith, Chavez, and Seaman (2012) identify and describe four major eras in education: (1) the Agricultural Age (1600s–mid-1800s), (2) the Industrial Age (mid-1800s–late 1990s), (3) the Information Age, or Digital Age (mid-1990s–early 2000s), and (4) the Conceptual Age (mid-2000s–present).

Education in the Agricultural Age in Colonial America was inconsistently available and often rudimentary, focused primarily on achieving basic literacy and numeracy. In addition, during much of this period education was not afforded to all students; that is, girls, minorities, and individuals with disabilities were often excluded from educational opportunities. The basic structures and systems of today's public education evolved during this time led by Horace Mann and others, and by the end of the Agricultural Age, public education based on an "age grade" system was established.

The Industrial Age marked a significant period of growth for public education, both at the K–12 and higher education levels. By 1918, every state had passed compulsory education laws and attendance was required at the elementary level. The system of administration, including school superintendents and school boards, was solidified at this time. An increased number of subject and content offerings came into existence, including art, music, clubs, other co-curricular activities, and athletics. After the launch of Sputnik in 1957, there was a renewed emphasis on science, math, and counseling to increase the capacity of the American workforce.

This period also saw increased funding and support in other areas of education as well in efforts to ensure that all children received a comprehensive education to maximize their skills and abilities. Vocational training efforts and funding expanded significantly during this period, especially in the 1960s. In 1975, PL94-142 Education for All Handicapped Children, also known as the Individuals with Disabilities Education Act, was passed, assuring much stronger educational rights for students with disabilities.

Throughout the twentieth century, public channels of communication were firmly established with newspaper circulation, radio, and television. In addition, personal means of communication also improved as phone and messaging systems became faster, clearer, and more complex. While these advancements improved access to information, it was not until computers and the Internet became widely available that the Information Age was ushered in around the mid-1990s. Suddenly, information stored in libraries or available through books, television, and/or radio was readily available anytime, anywhere.

Along with this increased access to information, education was experiencing increased federal and state accountability as the No Child Left Behind Act (NCLB) was passed in 2001. This act resulted in increased testing and accountability for student achievement as measured by standardized tests. NCLB created the framework for education for much of the Information Age.

Currently, education is moving from the Information Age to the Conceptual Age. That is, students no longer need teachers and schools to simply acquire information; they can get information anytime, anywhere, using computers, tablets, and cell phones. Schools are now being tasked with teaching competencies based largely on Common Core State Standards so that students know how to understand, process, use, synthesize, and create with the information that they can access. In the Conceptual Age, schools are offering a wider range of learning options for teachers, students, parents, school boards, and administrators, including charter schools, voucher schools, personalized learning environments, and blended classrooms. Most of these new classroom and school options rely significantly on technology and access to relevant content as well as scaffolded, purposeful knowledge and skill development.

The Conceptual Age is here and presents unique challenges and opportunities as boards and superintendents work to address student and staff needs in this new paradigm. School boards and superintendents must be familiar with the ways that technology can be integrated into instructional content and delivery to maximize student engagement and learning in today's educational environment. Board/superintendent teams will be tasked with making major policy decisions and resource allocations centered on the use of technology at the school and district levels. Issues boards and superintendents will be asked to consider include flipped classrooms, digital textbooks, 1:1 technology devices for students, the use of technology during nonschool hours, providing resources for students with limited or no resources in the home, and more.

WHAT IS NEEDED TO MAKE DISTRICTS TECHNOLOGICALLY COMPETITIVE

It is not enough to have the right tools and equipment, and it is not enough to have knowledgeable, trained, competent staff; schools must have both in order to deliver technology-based instructional models effectively and with fidelity.

Tools and Equipment. Perhaps the most important thing in making a school or district technologically literate is what no one ever sees: the infrastructure or network. Network capacity is finite and typically must be upgraded every five to ten years depending on the demands placed on it. Because it is not visible (for the most part), it can be tempting to let this piece slide when considering technology improvements in favor of more computers, tablets, printers, carts, and programs. However, when an overburdened system crashes (as it did at the start of the school year in one district), it can leave everyone without access for weeks and may require expensive experts and technicians for repair.

Care and maintenance of the system, as well as troubleshooting and technical support, are critical tools and equipment needed for a secure, legally compliant technology infrastructure. Regular backups of all school and district data, getting the right people access to the parts of the system within their authority, and fixing issues promptly are necessary to keep all educational and operational systems that rely on technology working properly.

Hardware and software must be available for teachers and students to implement technology-assisted or technology-based learning. Computers, tablets, SmartBoards, printers, cables, earphones, keyboards, and software are just some of the tools needed to facilitate technology in learning. This equipment and software has a limited lifespan, especially with regular daily use, so plans for updating and upgrading equipment must be built into the budget. The care and maintenance of this equipment must be arranged as well, including storage, use policies, check out procedures, and responsibility for care.

Building Staff Capacity. Taking full advantage of technology in instruction requires rethinking and expanding concepts of instructional delivery while incorporating what we already know about quality instruction into curriculum. Quality instruction using technology should include a variety of relevant and engaging content options, purposeful scaffolding to strengthen existing knowledge and skills and build new ones, and questions/tasks that incorporate lower- and higher-order thinking skills.

Accomplishing these goals requires building staff capacity so that they are knowledgeable about the possibilities that technology tools can provide, and they understand how to maximize the learning potential these tools can offer. Schools and districts are responsible for building technology capacity through purposeful, ongoing professional development to promote common concepts, vocabulary, and skill sets to build and implement effective technology-assisted or technology-based instructional models.

Professional development should be relevant and useable, sequenced and paced in a logical manner, and include opportunities for practice and implementation. Depending on the level of staff ability with technology (which is likely to include a wide range of abilities), a successful professional development plan may include different options for staff depending on their expertise with technology.

Staff capacity in technology-assisted or technology-based learning models, such as blended learning or personalized learning environments, requires not only technological capacity, but ultimately multiple pathways to student learning using a common language and common principles. Curriculum development in these models typically requires a high level of collaboration and professional development as educators learn how to incorporate multiple pathways into lesson plans. A fully realized twenty-first-century classroom model as it is conceptualized today requires creating rich, diverse content across a variety of platforms that enable students to control and customize their learning experiences while maintaining high levels of rigor, relevance, and developmentally appropriate content that meet state and national standards.

WHAT CAN BOARDS AND SUPERINTENDENTS DO TO FACILITATE TECHNOLOGY IN THE DISTRICT?

School boards typically approve technology plans for the district. These plans address, among other things, the integration of technology into the district and curriculum. Developing and maintaining a comprehensive plan is critical to managing the rapidly changing technology environment.

State and federal statutes articulate requirements that should be considered when building a technology plan, including the Children's Internet Protection Act (CIPA) (2000). In addition to these protection requirements, states typically articulate requirements for district technology plans. In Wisconsin, for example, each school district is required to file a technology plan with the Wisconsin Department of Public Instruction (DPI). These plans can be accessed at https://sites.google.com/a/dpi.wi.gov/wisconsin-technology-planning/school-and-district-plans.

Each technology plan must contain several required components. While the list below is state specific, it does include the fundamental components of a sound technology plan and would be an appropriate model to begin crafting a technology plan in any district:

- Home page, or introduction
- List of authors and approval documents
- A needs assessment
    - Look at last plan and data that you have collected and reflect on where you are.
    - Do you want to continue current goals, modify them, or add new ones?
- Goals
    - Goal 1: Student achievement
    - Goal 2: Effective teaching and learning practices
    - Goal 3: Access to information sources and learning tools
    - Goal 4: Support systems and leadership
- Action Plan
    - Objectives and action steps
    - Professional development
    - Infrastructure
    - Upgrades
    - Assessment measures
    - Evaluations
- Library Media Program
    - Required by the state and can be combined with the technology plan
- Monitoring and Updating
    - Yearly monitoring suggested
- Estimated Budget
    - Estimated costs with possible funding sources

- Data
  - Data related to readiness and capacity for technology-based implementations
- Policies
  - Include board policies relevant to technology issues
- Infrastructure
  - Resources and fixed assets
  - Software
  - Telecommunication and technology infrastructure
  - Phone
  - Website
- Curricular Alignment
  - Present curricular alignment with technology (integration)

Policies Related to Technology. The board's role in setting policy for technology use is critical. Such policies set the tone for how carefully technology is monitored, student, staff, and parent access, the district's Internet presence (including social media), and more. As school districts acquire more technological capacity and legal decisions about technology use and social media are clarified, the range of acceptable policy options for districts has increased over the last decade. That is, such policies are not one-size-fits-all propositions, and such policies should reflect the culture and values of a community.

While there is no set rule on the number or type of policies a district may have governing technology, certain "must have" policies are an expected part of the board policy manual. Below is a list of critical policies and the issues they should address:

- Acceptable Use Policy for Students and Staff
  - Sets the parameters for general, overall use of technology by students and staff
  - Establishes acceptable use policies and students' use of their own technology in school

- Establishes acceptable use of social media at school
- Establishes use of school technology outside school day
- Sets parameters for personal, nonwork-related usage
- Establishes procedures for appeal

- Technology Accommodations for Students with Disabilities

    - Complies with Section 504 of the Rehabilitation Act of 1973 and IDEA and other relevant state and federal statutes
    - Is usually crafted in collaboration with the special education staff

- District Web Pages

    - Provides required elements for district web pages, including templates
    - Establishes the degree of school autonomy and individuality in web page appearance and content
    - Establishes information guidelines for district web pages
    - Designates employee to update and monitor web-based content
    - Communicates process for selection and proofing of web-based content

- Copyright Policy

    - Articulates the protocols for district compliance with federal copyright law
    - Considers traditional photocopies as well as web-based nonoriginal content

TECHNOLOGY RESOURCES FOR BOARDS AND SUPERINTENDENTS

Two critical aspects of working with technology issues are understanding and using a common vocabulary. This common understanding can be a challenge because of the rapidly evolving nature of technology and the fact that some terms and concepts are general while others are specific to education.

The following lexicon is a quick reference to commonly used technology terms and concepts in education today. Each term contains a definition, the use of the term in a sentence to provide context for the reader, and a Quick Response (QR) code. The QR code provides a direct link to web-based content that provides more in-depth information about the term. The QR code can be used with a QR reader on a smart phone or tablet equipped with a camera. These apps are available very inexpensively for a wide variety of devices.

Using the QR code reader typically involves opening the app and taking a picture of the code. The QR reader then reads the code and redirects to the requested page. QR codes are designed for "on the go" use because they enable users to access information quickly without having to type in a web address.

The lexicon that follows this chapter is not exhaustive, but does provide foundational information that illustrates the expansion of technology terms and usage in education in recent years.

SUMMARY

School board members and superintendents must be familiar with the role technology plays in today's education. Clear evidence exists that technology and media-driven classroom environments are expanding at a rapid rate. Board members and superintendents will likely be tasked with making major policy decisions regarding the use of technology and the allocation of finances for such use.

ADDITIONAL MATERIALS

Technology Lexicon: A Primer for Educators

One to One Computing (1:1)

Most commonly refers to a program or initiative in which a school provides one device (for example, laptop, tablet, etc.) per student. This program is new but popular in many districts, and conflicting reports exist citing its advantages and disadvantages. Many PK–12 schools are currently running 1:1 pilots to test this initiative.

For example: Andy's school gave him an iPad to use for the entire school year as part of their 1:1 iPad initiative.

Adaptive Learning

An educational process in which the teaching methods and materials are adapted to each student's pace and level. Technology is often used in adaptive learning because software can be changed to provide different exercises, questions, and content based on student input.

For example: Jack is doing well with geometry, but getting many algebra questions wrong. As a result, the app he is using increases the difficulty of the geometry questions while presenting easier algebra questions to help him along.

Assistive Technology

Any piece of technology, hardware, or software that helps a person with disabilities perform everyday tasks that might otherwise be difficult or impossible. This technology can include everything from wheelchairs to screen readers to text telephones.

For example: Isabella is hearing impaired and turns on the captions of instructional YouTube videos to understand what is being said.

Augmentative and Alternative Communication (AAC)

Any communication method that helps individuals with speech and language impairments. AAC technologies are a subcategory of assistive technologies and include text-to-speech communicators and picture communicators.

For example: Holly has a speech impediment and uses AAC iPad apps to communicate. In

TECHNOLOGY IN SCHOOLS

these apps, she taps on pictures of words she wants to say and the app says the words out loud.

Big Data

A collection of data sets so large that specialized technologies, techniques, and technicians are required to process, manage, and store them. An industry has arisen around the processing and analysis of large volumes of student data.

For example: The state education agency collects, analyzes, and warehouses big data on student test scores, attendance, and economic conditions as a means of tracking student achievement throughout the state.

Blended Learning

A teaching practice that combines in-person and online instructional delivery. The instruction of a lesson occurs with both teacher interaction and computing devices. Also known as Hybrid Learning.

For example: Matias learns about algebra from his teacher, then goes to the computer lab to practice algebra questions using a math program.

Bring Your Own Device (BYOD)

Also known as Bring Your Own Technology (BYOT), an initiative in which students bring their own mobile devices into the classroom for class purposes, as opposed to using school-issued devices. BYOD is often seen as an alternative to 1:1 programs because of lower maintenance costs, although students without devices cannot participate.

For example: Li Ting brings her Android phone to class every day for use as a clicker because of her school's BYOD program. (*See* Clickers.)

Clickers

A device or mobile app that allows students to answer closed-ended items. Multiple-choice questions, true-false items, yes-no items, and voting are examples of the ways teachers can use these clickers and apps. The results of clicker responses can be shown immediately to students while maintaining student anonymity to alleviate anxiety about wrong responses.

For example: Mr. Shah asked his class a multiple-choice question and all students in the class answered by pressing a button on their clicker device. The answers were instantly recorded by the app and the results were visible on the SmartBoard.

Cloud

A generic term used to represent the concept of distributed computing in which a set of networked computers allow for shared services. Also used synonymously with the Internet.

For example: The AP English class study group set up an account on Google Docs so that they could work collaboratively on their final project from their homes through the cloud.

Digital Classroom

A classroom that mostly or entirely relies on electronic devices and software instead of paper and pens. A central computing device, like a laptop or tablet, typically characterizes a digital classroom.

For example: Justin uses a Google Chromebook for all of his reading, research, assignments, and other individualized work at any time because his teacher set up a paperless, digital classroom.

Digital Native

An individual born during or after the common use of digital technologies, such as the Internet, mobile devices, and apps. It is assumed that such individuals have a strong grasp of digital technology because it has always been part of their lives.

For example: Robin was born in 2001 and is a digital native because extensive technology has been available during her lifetime.

Education Technology

Any kind of technology used for educational purposes by an educator or educational institution. Most commonly used in reference to software utilized in primary, secondary, and higher education, although it can cover much more than that. Also known as "edtech."

For example: Camille is playing with an educational phonics game on her iPad. The company that makes this game is an edtech company.

Edupunk

An attitude in which learning can happen on one's own without any formal structure. Often described as "do-it-yourself (DIY) education." Interestingly, the originator of this term, Jim Groom, no longer calls himself an edupunk.

For example: Frank is an edupunk because he creates his own curriculum from the material he has available to him rather than paying for commercial products.

Flipped Classroom

The practice of engaging in the initial learning outside of the regular classroom and reinforcing the learning with activities in the classroom. Flipped learning is conceptually opposed to traditional learning, in which the initial learning is done in the classroom and reinforced with homework. Flipped classroom concepts lend themselves well to blended learning if the technology is available to all students outside the classroom.

For example: Chloe watched several calculus videos at home to learn the calculus equations, then came to class and worked on calculus questions with a group of classmates. When she got stuck, she collaborated with her group members and the teacher.

Gamification

The practice of incorporating game mechanics into an activity. Examples of game mechanics are goals, badges, competition, immediate feedback, and leveling up.

For example: Mrs. McSweeney gamified her classroom by awarding badges for reaching achievement levels.

Hybrid Learning

See Blended Learning.

Instructional Technology

A subset of educational technology, this practice focuses more on the use of technology for instructional purposes, though the terms are sometimes used interchangeably.

For example: Mr. Garcia designs and builds courseware tools in his role as an instructional technologist.

Information Technology (IT)

A general term referring to the operational and instructional technology infrastructures in a district. IT is built on a system or platform that is largely password protected, safeguarded, and regularly backed up. The IT system is the basis of virtually all critical information systems in a modern school district.

For example: The IT director is responsible for maintaining all technology systems and information in the district.

Learning Management System (LMS)

A piece of software that manages, analyzes, and interfaces educational courses and training programs. Learning management systems can also be used to manage course registration, curriculum, skill and competencies, and report generation. Most modern LMS packages are web-based.

For example: Ms. Kensington is deciding between Moodle, Blackboard, Desire2Learn, and Schoology for managing her teachers' curriculum materials and students' assessments.

Massive Open Online Course (MOOC)

An online course that includes video lectures, reading materials, problem sets, and a student community. Supporters see MOOCs as a disruptive innovation and detractors question its actual educational efficacy. MOOCs are typically free; however, no credit is associated with them.

For example: Maddy has been taking a computer programming MOOC with Coursera at night with the hopes of improving her computing skills and changing careers one day.

Open Educational Resource (OER)

Any online educational material freely accessible and openly licensed for public consumption. Such materials can be online courses, lectures, homework assignments, exercises, quizzes, interactive simulations, and games.

For example: Mrs. Sekibo is putting together her lesson plan by searching the web for OER materials she can include.

Open Source Software

Any piece of software freely available and openly licensed. Other programmers can contribute to the original software or create their own versions of it. Most modern websites incorporate some kind of open source software.

For example: Being a starving student, Jorge uses free open source software to run his blog. He sometimes writes new code and gives it back to the original blog programmers.

Personal Learning Network (PLN)

An informal network of people professional in nature and meant to aid an educator in furthering his/her pedagogical craft. Because teaching in a classroom does not lend itself to a great deal of peer interaction, teachers create PLNs to connect with other teachers for advice and support.

For example: Mr. Wayne grows his PLN through social media sites like Twitter and Tumblr.

Student Information System (SIS)

A piece of software that manages student data. This management includes grades, attendance, background information, discipline records, and health records.

For example: As the school counselor, Mr. Rankin uses the district's SIS to access Joey's disciplinary record.

REFERENCE

Smith, S., Chavez, A., and Seaman, G. (2012). *Teacher as architect*. Chicago, IL: Modern Teacher Press.

RESOURCES

7

ADMINISTRATIVE ASSISTANTS

A Critical Resource
Bette A. Lang and Thomas F. Evert

The partnership between the superintendent and her or his administrative assistant is critical and dynamic. In countless school districts and offices across the country each day, the administrative assistant is the pivotal staff member in determining the workflow and efficiency of the organization.

A key role the administrative assistant plays, which is usually informal and often unrecognized, is as the superintendent's liaison to a wide range of internal and external audiences. The administrative assistant is the indispensable link between the board, superintendent, district employees, parents, various community leaders, and a wide range of out-of-district connections.

The administrative assistant is also the human processor of time demands for the superintendent. The administrative assistant can determine through questioning if individuals could be better served with another resource person, and whether they will be amenable to seeing someone other than the superintendent. With consultation and awareness of priorities, administrative assistants are able to determine the most efficient use of their superintendents' time. Time spent briefing administrative assistants on issues and priorities reap great benefits in the form of an efficient and positive working environment and sound public relations.

Another key characteristic of highly capable administrative assistants is an exceptional work ethic coupled with a giving and caring attitude. These individuals anticipate situations, arrive early, and are always willing to stay until the last "rush job" is completed.

Administrative assistants not only serve the superintendent, but also serve the board. These individuals may be board clerks, the superintendent's personal administrative assistant, or another designated individual. However the role is titled, these individuals do for the board what the superintendent's administrative assistant does for the superintendent. Using and managing this resource wisely goes a long way to an efficient and effective board, particularly in the areas of scheduling and communication.

An excellent and detailed resource about the role of administrative assistants is found in the National School Boards Association (NASB) guidebook (2006), which highlights specific responsibilities for administrative assistants. The superintendent and administrative assistant develop and implement systems for (a) informing board members on operational matters, (b) preparing board packets and communications, (c) implementing phone trees, and (d) receiving and sending e-mails and memos. A key aspect of the administrative assistant/superintendent relationship is to have a high level of agreement about how all of these systems are implemented.

An important feature of determining parameters for the board and superintendent is to clearly define the school district management/leadership team (NASB, 2006). The definition will be determined in part by the style of the board president and superintendent, size of the district, and the history of the district.

Eadie (2007) writes of the belief that behind every successful nonprofit board (including a school board) is a "board-savvy CEO" (p. 28). He stresses the need for executive support of the CEO, which includes tasks typically completed by the administrative assistant such as preparation of materials, compiling reports, and scheduling the CEO's time.

Kersten's advice to beginning school administrators provides support related to the important role of the administrative assistant (2010). He addresses the importance of office staff as well as the importance of administrators working together for a common cause.

WHAT BOARD PRESIDENTS, SUPERINTENDENTS, AND ADMINISTRATIVE ASSISTANTS HAVE TO SAY

Survey Overview. The authors (two former superintendents and one superintendent administrative assistant) asked a variety of board presidents, superintendents, and administrative assistants in Wisconsin about their views on the roles and value of the administrative assistants to the school district. Survey respondents were from one of three Cooperative Educational Service Agency (CESA) regions representing the southeast, western, and north central areas of the state. The survey was administered electronically and sent to 162 superintendents. The superintendents were asked to forward the survey on to board presidents and administrative assistants. Respondents were primarily located in districts serving fewer than five thousand students.

Demographics. The number of respondents was almost equal for superintendents and administrative assistants with thirty-seven superintendents and thirty-four administrative assistants. Only one-third as many board presidents ($n = 10$) responded. Most respondents were from districts with fewer than 1,499 students. Thus, any generalized statements regarding findings should be considered in light of district size.

The administrative assistants had more experience in their respective positions in the district than superintendents or board presidents. A possible explanation is that board presidents and superintendents are more tenuous political leadership positions than administrative assistants. Board presidents were almost evenly split between baby boomers (born 1946–1964) and Generation X (born 1965–1982). Administrative assistants and superintendents shared similar generational demographics, with roughly two-thirds from each group being boomers and roughly one-third Generation X. This distribution may indicate the longevity needed to "get to the top of the profession" for both administrative assistants and superintendents.

Communication. Administrative assistants' communication responsibilities were ranked high by both superintendents and board presidents with administrative assistants ranking communication the highest of all respondents for all four groups: board, superintendent, administrators, and the public as shown in table 7.1.

Table 7.1. Importance of Administrative Assistants' Communication Responsibilities

	AA's COMMUNICATION WITH:	BOARD PRESIDENT Responses n = 10	ADMINISTRATIVE ASSISTANT Responses n = 34	SUPERINTENDENT Responses n = 37
1	Board	M = 4.6 Range = 3–5	M = 4.6 Range = 1–5	M = 4.5 Range = 2–5
2	Superintendent	M = 4.9 Range = 4–5	M = 5.0 Range = 5	M = 4.9 Range = 4–5
3	Administrators	M = 4.6 Range = 3–5	M = 4.8 Range = 4–5	M = 4.3 Range = 3–5
4	Public	M = 4.0 Range = 1–5	M = 4.5 Range = 3–5	M = 4.2 Range = 1–5

Note: 5 = Very Important; 1 = Not Important. M = Mean, Total n = 81 respondents

Board presidents' responses indicated the most important communication responsibilities an administrative assistant had was with the superintendent. The next most important communication responsibilities were with the board and other administrators equally. Least important for administrative assistants regarding communication was the public.

Clearly board presidents perceive the superintendent/administrative assistant communication as most important. Superintendents also view superintendent/administrative assistant communication as the most important. They view administrative assistants' communication with the board as second highest in importance followed by communication with administrators and the public.

Administrative assistants view the importance of administrative assistant/superintendent communication as the most important. In fact, administrative assistants gave all 5.0 (highest values) to this area. Second most important were administrators, third the board, and last the public. These results can facilitate effective dialogue between boards, superintendents, and administrative assistants because these communications are so critical to effective board governance. The superintendents who participated in this survey shared this view.

Perceptions of How Administrative Assistants Spend Their Time. Administrative assistants were asked to report how they spend their time, while board presidents and superintendents were asked about how they perceive that administrative assistants spend their time. The results of this survey item are presented in table 7.2.

Table 7.2. Respondents' Perceptions of Administrative Assistants' Time Allocation on Specific Tasks

	Specific Tasks	BOARD PRESIDENT Responses n = 10	ADMINISTRATIVE ASSISTANT Responses n = 34	SUPERINTENDENT Responses n = 37
1	Preparing board packets	M = 3.3 Range = 2–5	M = 3.3 Range = 1–5	M = 3.0 Range = 1–5
2	Communication with public	M = 2.9 Range = 1–4	M = 3.5 Range = 1–5	M = 3.5 Range = 2–5
3	Schedule appointments for superintendent	M = 3.0 Range = 1–4	M = 3.0 Range = 1–5	M = 3.7 Range = 2–5
4	Communication with board member	M = 3.6 Range = 3–5	M = 4.0 Range = 2–5	M = 3.5 Range = 1–5
5	Word processing	M = 4.3 Range = 3–5	M = 4.5 Range = 1–5	M = 3.0 Range = 1–5
6	Communication with district employees	M = 4.0 Range = 3–5	M = 3.6 Range = 2–5	M = 2.7 Range = 1–5

Note: 5 = Very Important; 1 = Not Important. M = Mean, Total n = 81 respondents

Table 7.2 shows that board presidents believe administrative assistants spend their time in the following ways, in rank order: word processing activities first, communication with district employees second, and communication with the board third. The three lowest ranked tasks in terms of time on task, according to board presidents, were preparing board packets, scheduling appointments for superintendents, and communication with the public.

Administrative assistants were in agreement with board presidents regarding the highest ranked activity in terms of time spent: word processing tasks. Communication with board members was second and communication with district employees third. The administrative assistants' lowest three rankings were communication with public, preparing board packets, and scheduling the superintendent's time.

Interestingly, superintendent perceptions and administrative assistants' reported time on tasks varied a great deal. First, superintendents perceived that administrative assistants spent the most time on scheduling and the next most time on communications with board members and the public. While board presidents and administrative assistants perceived word processing as the most time-intensive activity in which administrative assistants engaged, word processing was tied for fourth by superintendents along with preparing board packets. Superintendents perceived administrative assistants as spending time with district employees as the activity that involved the least amount of time.

This difference in how the three groups view administrative assistants as spending their time could be a worthy topic for an administrative assistant, board president, and superintendent discussion. It is always helpful when individuals who work so closely together have a clear understanding of workload, roles and responsibilities of each position, and the time needed to complete various tasks in each position.

WHAT ADVICE WOULD BOARD PRESIDENTS GIVE TO ADMINISTRATIVE ASSISTANTS?

The survey included several open-ended items to ask administrative assistants, board presidents, and superintendents about advice and suggestions.

Board presidents were asked if they had any advice for administrative assistants. Several board presidents stated their appreciation for administrative assistants and encouraged the need for ongoing communication. Because the administrative assistant serves the superintendent directly and the board indirectly, the comments received were understandably not specific in nature.

Following are the summary statements of board presidents' advice to administrative assistants:

- Keep up the good work you are already doing (seven responses)
- Communicate with the board and in general (two responses)
- Prioritize and delegate if possible (one response)

WHAT ADVICE WOULD ADMINISTRATIVE ASSISTANTS GIVE BOARD PRESIDENTS?

Most important, administrative assistants want board presidents to be clear and direct in their communication with them. Administrative assistants stated they want to be helpful to board presidents and that the best way to do so is for board presidents to clearly communicate what they and the board need.

The role of the administrative assistant is varied. It is obvious that the clearer the role expectations on the part of the board president, the better. We encourage administrative assistants, board presidents, and superintendents to have this dialogue.

Following is a summary of administrative assistants' advice to board presidents:

- Communication, be direct, clear, ask how can I help, remind the rest of board of their role (fourteen responses)
- Don't micromanage the superintendent (four responses)
- Have a good relationship with superintendent (three responses)
- Copy me on communication with superintendent (two responses)
- There were thirteen other areas (thirteen responses) including:
  - Don't backstab me
  - Be reachable at all times
  - Check messages
  - Plan ahead
  - Set board agenda meetings

WHAT ADVICE WOULD ADMINISTRATIVE ASSISTANTS GIVE SUPERINTENDENTS?

Administrative assistants were asked about advice they would give to superintendents. It comes as no surprise that administrative assistants want the same thing from superintendents that they want from board presidents: clear communication! In fact, several administrative assistants wrote of the need for superintendents to make communication with the administrative assistant a top priority. Closely related to the need for good overall communication, administrative assistants encouraged superintendents to "keep them in the loop" and provide "heads-up" alerts for anticipated difficult situations and urgent work requests.

Following are summary comments from administrative assistants relative to their advice to superintendents:

- Communicate on a regular basis, make administrative assistant communication with superintendent a top priority (seventeen responses)
- Give administrative assistants "heads-up" alerts, keep in loop (seven responses)
- Need to prioritize, can't do all at once (three responses)
- Have unconditional trust (three responses)
- There were eight other areas (eight responses) including:
  - Manage all employees
  - Need PR budget
  - Give praise
  - Provide team spirit
  - Keep posted about board activities

WHAT ADVICE WOULD SUPERINTENDENTS GIVE TO ADMINISTRATIVE ASSISTANTS?

Superintendents largely agreed that administrative assistants and superintendents should have open communication, trust, and regular meetings. Superintendents also indicated that they sought out administrative assistants who possessed specific character traits, including sincerity, approachability, being a good listener, and having a good sense of humor. Of almost equal importance was the need for the administrative assistant to do quality work as a result of being organized, attending to details, and setting goals. Superintendents also appear to value confidentiality, time management skills, and administrative assistants who are in touch with district happenings.

A tall order? Indeed. Superintendents advise administrative assistants to demonstrate a wide array of skills, including effective communications, excellent interpersonal skills, technical proficiency, and yes, even clairvoyance!

Following is the summary of superintendents' advice to administrative assistants:

- Work closely with superintendent, open communication, trust with superintendent, meet regularly (nine responses)

- Have these personal characteristics (nine responses):
  - Be sincere
  - Be approachable
  - Good listener
  - Sense of humor
- Do quality work (eight responses) including:
  - Be organized
  - Have attention to detail
  - Have good secretarial skills
  - Be able to prioritize and set goals
- Serve as confidential sounding board (four responses)
- Time management skills (four responses)
- Know what's happening in district (four responses)
- Establish working relationship with all groups (three responses)

WHAT TRAINING/PROFESSIONAL DEVELOPMENT TOPICS DO ADMINISTRATIVE ASSISTANTS BELIEVE WOULD BEST IMPROVE THEIR JOB PERFORMANCE?

Administrative assistants listed a wide variety of topics for training and professional development that they would like to attend. Topics are listed below.

- Advanced technology/social media training (thirteen responses)
- Communication opportunities with other administrative assistants (six responses)
- Legislative and legal updates (six responses)
- Techniques for communicating with difficult people (four responses)
- Stress reduction techniques, leadership training (one response each)

WHAT TRAINING/PROFESSIONAL DEVELOPMENT TOPICS DO SUPERINTENDENTS BELIEVE WOULD BEST IMPROVE ADMINISTRATIVE ASSISTANTS' JOB PERFORMANCE?

Superintendents believe administrative assistants should engage in a wide range of professional development activities. Interestingly, superintendents indicated the need for legal professional development, a topic not mentioned in depth by the administrative assistants themselves.

- Legal issues, open records/meetings laws, policies (nine responses)
- Network with other administrative assistants, state conferences (eight responses)
- Technology seminars and software training (five responses)
- Communication skills/strategies, conflict resolution (five responses)
- State accountability reports (two responses)

WHAT ASPECTS OF THEIR JOBS DO ADMINISTRATIVE ASSISTANTS LIKE THE MOST AND THE LEAST?

Overall, administrative assistants like or love their jobs. The wide range of tasks, the variety of work, and the fact that every day is busy all appeal to administrative assistants. Administrative assistants have immense pride in their work, want to do exceedingly well, and believe their role is important. They want students to succeed and the district to thrive.

The following are responses from administrative assistants as to which aspects of their jobs they like the most and which aspects they like the least:

Administrative Assistants: What Aspect of Your Job do You Most Like?

- Wide variety of work, every day is different, different tasks, always learning (thirteen responses)
- Like/love all of it (six responses)
- Importance and responsibility of role (three responses)
- Working with students (three responses)
- Public relations (two responses)

- Answering wide range of questions quickly and efficiently (two responses)
- There were nine other areas (nine responses) including:
  - Independence
  - Working with superintendent
  - Networking
  - Seeing student progress
  - Work with board
  - Elections

Administrative Assistants: What Aspect of Your Job do You Like Least?

- To be last in communication loop, then have to rush to finish job (three responses)
- New technology (three responses)
- The politics, controversies (three responses)
- State accountability reports (two responses)
- Repetitive work (two responses)
- Friction between board and superintendent (two responses)
- Other responses (fifteen responses) including:
  - Listen to public
  - Try to schedule board committee meetings
  - Expulsions
  - Lack of time
  - Seeing district misrepresented
  - Parent issues
  - Taking minutes at board meetings
  - No time to file
  - Referendum
  - Long hours/night meetings

SUMMARY

Administrative assistants are a critical resource to superintendents and board presidents.

The most common and recurring theme reported by all three groups was the need for open and direct communication between administrative assistants, board presidents, and superintendents. Most pointedly, administrative assistants want to know as much as possible about what board presidents and superintendents need from them. Both administrative assistants and superintendents believe that administrative assistants should engage in professional development on a variety of relevant topics, including aspects of the law that touch the administrative assistant's position. Administrative assistants generally enjoy their work, especially the variety and value they bring to the district.

Note: Sincere thanks to the individuals who served in the administrative assistant capacity during our tenures as superintendents. They had many responsibilities, such as the job of orientating us to the district, managing the environment in the superintendent's office, catching all of the things that might have fallen by the wayside, and being the first voice people heard when contacting the superintendent's office. Mere words cannot express our gratitude to Carol, Charlotte, Diane, Gwen, Karen, Michelle, Peg, and Wanda!

REFERENCES

Eadie, D. (2007). *Meeting the governing challenge: Applying the high impact governing model to your organization* (1st ed.). Governance Edge Publications.

Kersten, T. A. (2010). *Stepping into administration: How to succeed in making the move.* Lanham, MD: Rowman & Littlefield.

National School Boards Association. (2006). *Becoming a better board member: A guide to effective school board service* (3rd ed.). Alexandria, VA: National School Boards Association.

8

USING EXTERNAL EXPERTS FOR DISTRICT IMPROVEMENT

Thomas F. Evert and Amy E. Van Deuren

Hiring, working with, and evaluating external experts or consultants can be a challenge for boards and superintendents. This chapter provides a brief overview on the use of consultants and practical suggestions boards and superintendents can consider when employing a consultant or external expert. In addition, using consultants to address board and superintendent professional development is addressed.

DeWitt (2013) discusses the need to be "consultant savvy." DeWitt mentioned that the No Child Left Behind (NCLB) legislation helped create a need for increased use of consultants. He added that a wide range of consultant skill levels exists. Boards and superintendents must determine the level and type of expertise they desire and search for the right match when selecting a consultant.

DeWitt focused a great deal on the role of the consultant and provided applied and common sense advice for individuals serving as consultants to school districts. Specific advice included dealing with the natural resistance that will likely be experienced when a consultant is hired. The consultant must be engaging and not aloof, and address the need for objectivity as much as possible. DeWitt also stressed the importance of a consultant being timely, such as arriving early for district work, and successfully completing assigned tasks. Each of these factors was combined with the importance of the consultant being knowledgeable in his or her area of expertise.

DeWitt also highlighted the need for boards and superintendents to be cautious and savvy regarding the expense of a consultant. The need to consider political factors and environments was also a consideration in the task of selecting a consultant. The bottom line: consultant skills and service offerings vary greatly, and boards and superintendents must do their homework when determining the purpose and employment of a consultant. DeWitt stressed that many times consultants were indeed helpful in the attempts to improve districts.

STUDENT AND DISTRICT NEEDS

An important part of selecting a consultant or external expert is for the board and superintendent to know and understand the needs of the district. Boards and superintendents must assess where the district is in terms of achievement levels, financial status, student service needs, leadership issues, and curriculum development and delivery. In addition to having a realistic and accurate understanding of current needs, boards and superintendents should include other assessments as part of a pre-consultant selection process. Some important factors to be considered are the district history and culture, level of community support, parent involvement, and student and teacher characteristics such as test scores, learning goals, poverty level, and teacher quality.

Three additional areas where external experts have been valuable are district student population projections, purchasing health insurance, and assessing and addressing facility needs, including energy management and referendum planning. These three areas use common practices such as determining a district committee with representation from specific areas, examining the need or interest of the district, preparing the specific work tasks, and parameters and methods of hiring an external expert. Once the hiring decision is made, establishing a schedule of work and timelines will help provide the accountability and evaluation checkpoints necessary to ensure return on investment. In addition, boards and superintendents may want to examine any opportunities for establishing in-house experts who are trained by the external expert to continue the role of addressing the need after the external expert's contract is completed.

A DISTRICT CASE HISTORY

Regardless of the size of the district, boards and superintendents will usually employ consultants in two very important areas: law and finance. It is strongly suggested that a district have clear policies, guidelines, and regulations for the hiring, monitoring, and evaluation of legal and financial consultants. Evert and Van Deuren (2012) use material from a detailed case history to analyze the experiences of how one district used financial and legal consultants over a thirteen-year period.

Legal Advisors. Most districts employ an attorney on a regular retainer to serve as the attorney for the district or school. Typically, this attorney advises the superintendent, and on occasion both the board and superintendent. During Evert's fourteen-year tenure as superintendent of a ten-thousand-student district, he had the opportunity to work with three very qualified school attorneys. Each demonstrated a number of strengths.

The first two school attorneys served for nine years each and the third continues to serve with a new superintendent. The district had a hiring procedure that allowed any attorney in the county to apply for the position every three years and then a committee comprised of one board member, the superintendent, and a human resource staff member made the final hiring decision. One of the factors strongly considered was that the attorney had backup support from his or her law firm.

The school attorney handles a wide range of duties and frequently confers with and advises the superintendent on a variety of topics and issues. Situations or examples for which the superintendent may seek advice include dicey personnel issues, student suspension or expulsion questions, board policy, and administrative regulation development or interpretation. The school attorney may also participate in teacher negotiations, or the board may hire an attorney specialist to help negotiate teacher contracts. Some districts hire an attorney outside the district who specializes in collective bargaining to negotiate for reasons of expertise and politics.

It is important that the school attorney and superintendent develop a system of prioritizing communications and ensuring that responses are timely. Besides teacher negotiations, boards and superintendents may also have a need to hire specific legal services for real estate issues, personnel issues, and special education cases.

Often, legal counsel represents both the board and superintendent. However, there are times where there may be a need for both the board and superintendent to have separate legal representation. The board and superintendent should agree on how to accomplish the assigning of counsel should each entity need separate representation.

Financial Advisors. Financial advisors are frequently needed when districts address loan repayments and structure referendum questions. Financial decisions are critical, and it is very important to receive sound financial advice from proven experts in school finance. Very few board members and superintendents have the background or understanding to make recommendations regarding loans and loan repayments, interest rates, and investments. Decisions in these areas can save or cost the district significant amounts of money, and can involve potential legal disputes.

Superintendents and board members, especially in smaller districts, are often called upon to complete state education department financial requirements and documentation themselves, without in-depth training and/or a financial background. Computing levy rates, fund balances, and other critical data requires precise understanding of the calculations involved. External experts and state department of education websites can be particularly helpful for those who serve in districts without business directors or comptroller services.

When hiring a financial consultant, consider their area of expertise, including licenses and credentials. Financial consultants who work with school districts frequently work with more than one and will have references. Consider the amount of work they are being asked to do, the length of time they have to do it, and how often throughout the school year their services might be needed. Financial consultants, like attorneys, are often highly specialized, with expertise areas including referendum funding, bond sale coordination, pension liabilities, debt consolidation, and debt payoff schedules.

BOARD AND SUPERINTENDENT PROFESSIONAL DEVELOPMENT

An often-overlooked and neglected area of consultant services is that of providing professional development for boards and superintendents. A board/superintendent team may overlook the need for their joint professional growth. Marzano and Waters (2009) have provided a framework of leadership advice that can be useful for boards and superintendents as they plan and participate in their professional development.

A general board/superintendent discussion regarding their professional development is encouraged before hiring an external expert. The expert should be hired to target specific areas for growth, which may include communication, decision making, long-range planning, goal setting, and other issues of high interest and/or need identified by the board/superintendent team. Marzano and Waters (2009) stressed the need for boards and superintendents to keep the big picture in mind and to stay focused on the purpose for which a consultant is hired.

It is important to recognize that professional development is more effective when boards and superintendents are on the same page and heading in the same direction. Differences of opinion should be addressed in a civil and respectful manner. Board and superintendent teams should learn how to engage each other to address conflicts and differences of opinion in a manner that facilitates the work of the district. An external expert can often assist with this process.

External experts can help move the district forward faster than it might otherwise, especially regarding new initiatives. However, initiative fatigue can set in if too many initiatives are started at once (Marzano and Waters, 2009). Reeves (2010) also addresses the need to pace initiatives. Time is fixed. Financial resources are usually fixed or diminishing, and emotional energy is variable, but has limits. Employees, although resilient, can be pushed to a point of diminishing returns. External experts can make efforts more efficient and effective, but cannot create time, energy, and resources where they do not initially exist.

LOGISTICS

Here are a few rules of thumb to consider when hiring an external expert:

Do Not Apologize. Boards and superintendents should not apologize for using a consultant to help them with determining district direction and board and/or superintendent improvement. The consultant can best serve the district when the board and superintendent provide pro and con feedback on ideas, keep the big picture in mind, and do not undermine district planning processes, including long-range or strategic planning.

Hire. Once the board and superintendent have agreed on the need for improvement through the use of an external expert, the logistics of hiring the individual or individuals can be addressed. General guidelines for boards/superintendent teams to consider include a commitment to funding (yes, experts cost money!), providing general guidelines for questions, determining who will conduct the interviews, completing reference checks, and keeping the board informed of overall progress (Evert and Van Deuren 2012).

Questions. Specific questions to ask an external expert focus on the training, level of expertise, track record (if any), and assessments/evaluation processes used to determine effectiveness. If more than one expert is being considered, the comparison of fee schedules, timelines, expenditures, qualifications, availability, and compatibility may help drive the selection process.

Money Challenge. In our ever-increasing era of accountability, boards and superintendents receive much scrutiny over the expenditures of district funds. This scrutiny is especially evident in areas that vocal and questioning members of the public may deem as nonessential expenditures. These individuals frequently view external experts as nonessential costs. Boards and superintendents must have answers ready to address the challenges of expenditures for experts. The experts may be considered a limited expenditure or ongoing annual expense, and this parameter should be clearly stated at the start of the process.

SUMMARY

Board members and superintendents can benefit from the objective, impartial view an external expert can offer. Experts can assist boards and superintendents in providing more effective services to districts. Consultants or external experts bring knowledge and wisdom to the table that can help the district in a wide variety of ways. Districts are strongly encouraged to be transparent, businesslike, and nonapologetic in determining and implementing expert services. Students, staff, boards, and the community can reap positive benefits.

REFERENCES

Dewitt, P. (2013). Schools need to be more consultant savvy. *Education Week Blogs*. July 22. Retrieved from http://www.edweek.org/ew/section/blogs/index.html.

Evert, T. F., and Van Deuren, A. E. (2012). *Making external experts work: Solutions for district leaders*. Lanham, MD: Rowman & Littlefield.

Marzano, R. J., and Waters, T. (2009). *District leadership that works: Striking the right balance*. Bloomington, IN: Solution Tree.

Reeves, D. (2010). *Transforming professional development into student results*. Alexandria, VA: Association for Supervision & Curriculum Development.

9

STATE AND NATIONAL ASSOCIATIONS, EXTERNAL EXPERTS, SEARCH FIRMS, AND UNIVERSITIES

Thomas F. Evert and Bette A. Lang

There are a number of resources for information school board members and superintendents can use to assist with a variety of issues, including the improvement of student learning and achievement and establishing and maintaining productive board/superintendent interactions. The cost of the resources provided in this chapter varies widely from little to no cost to significant expense. The chapter is *not* intended to be inclusive but rather to demonstrate what is available to boards and superintendents seeking information and resources and for those considering the use of a state or national association, consultant, search firm, or university resource. The goal of this chapter is to provide valuable and timely information, which can serve as a springboard to help connect boards and superintendents to very important and pertinent resources.

STATE-LEVEL INFORMATION

School board and superintendent associations are available in every state. Each association has a somewhat unique model that enables boards and superintendents to learn from and grow in understanding of state-level direction and dynamics. Presented is an example of the depth and breadth of resources available in Colorado, a state that provides comprehensive information that is typically available in other states as well.

Colorado is typical in that there are separate organizations for school boards and superintendents; however, both boards and superintendents can benefit by being familiar with the resources available from both sources. For the purpose of this chapter, the organizations will be considered together.

The Colorado board and superintendent associations included information in eight major areas:

1. *Vision, mission of boards, and superintendents:* The Colorado Association of School Boards (CASB) provides a clear, brief mission statement: "Advancing excellence in public education through effective leadership by locally elected boards of education." A vision statement could not be found on the website. The Colorado Association of Executives (CASE) is organized as a statewide umbrella association serving seven job-alike departments, one of which is the Association of Superintendents/Senior Administrators (CASSA). CASE/CASSA provides clear and brief vision and mission statements. CASSA places special emphasis on promoting visionary leadership in a global, competitive world.
2. *Duties of boards and superintendents:* In describing the roles of boards and superintendents, CASB stresses advocacy with local board involvement. CASB provides an extensive service guide covering nine areas from communication to policy services to superintendent searches to professional development. The CASE is composed of seven groups: (1) elementary principals, (2) secondary principals, (3) leaders in educational technology, (4) personnel administrators, (5) superintendents/senior administrators, (6) educational specialists, and (7) business officials. Each group has its own department and database along with an elected legal governing board. Membership in the organization is required to access resources.
3. *Expectations boards may have for superintendents and expectations superintendents may have for boards:* Expectations of school board/superintendent relationships are key to establishing and

maintaining a productive board/superintendent partnership. Expectations are useful in implementing roles and responsibilities listed in job descriptions. Board expectations for superintendents, as listed on the website in 2013, include the following areas: communication, relationships, student achievement, district leadership, decision making, and miscellaneous. There are 109 personal qualities, skills, and experiences deemed to be essential to the success of a district's future superintendent. Superintendent expectations for boards are not addressed.

4. *Guidelines for hiring a superintendent:* Both CASB and CASE/CASSA provide hiring and evaluation guidelines. CASB lists six points to "uniquely guide and assist" local boards in superintendent searches. These points include knowing Colorado and its politics and issues that affect education and being committed to the long-term success of the district. CASE/CASSA focuses on modeling the highest moral and ethical behavior in superintendents and superintendent candidates who are seeking positions.

5. *Evaluation guidelines of superintendents from boards and superintendents:* The CASB provides a sample policy for superintendent evaluations, while the CASE/CASSA provides information regarding personal and professional development opportunities to improve, enhance, and address areas included on a typical superintendent job description and evaluation.

6. *Board/superintendent relations, communications, and interactions:* The importance of board/superintendent relations, communications, and interactions are emphasized by the CASB's five-point strategy for developing a communication plan. One of these strategies affects board/superintendent communications: creating two to three talking points on an issue for district leaders to use when speaking about this issue. The CASE/CASSA mentions facilitating communication among educational leaders as a major focus of the organization.

7. *Guidelines for conflict resolution between boards and superintendents:* An area of interest to both boards and superintendents is conflict resolution. The CASB offers legal services addressing disciplinary hearings on employee conduct; however, the CASE/CASSA provides legal assistance but does not list resources to address conflict resolution.

8. *Professional development opportunities, especially joint ventures:* Professional development resources and materials are prominent on both the CASB and CASE/CASSA websites. The CASB provides an extensive leadership development program for board members. An online academy as well as state and regional conferences and workshops are listed. Support for board training is exemplified by the following statement from the website: "Colorado Association of School Boards provides opportunities for growth and skill building to board members and superintendents at every experience level." Strategic planning workshops and services for local districts are also available. The CASE/CASSA website emphasizes professional development as well as collaboration among the seven administrative groups it represents.
9. *Other:* In addition to the areas mentioned, CASB provides an extensive clipping service highlighting news articles reported from around the state in the past week. Job announcements of specific superintendent vacancies are included. In addition, a thirteen-page services guide addresses advocacy, communications, health benefits, legal and policy services, school board training, superintendent searches, strategic planning, and workshops and retreats. The CASE/CASSA has been in existence since 1969 and is governed by a seventeen-member Coordinating Council made up of representatives from each group it represents and the CASE president, past president, and president-elect.

NATIONAL ASSOCIATIONS

There are two long-standing, traditional, and highly recognized national associations representing school boards and superintendents. The National School Boards Association (NSBA) was founded in 1940 and is headquartered at the following address:

National School Boards Association
1680 Duke Street
Alexandria, VA 22314
1-800-669-0071

Many board members, school districts, and central office staff subscribe to the monthly edition of the *American School Board Journal: The Source for School Leaders.*

The American Association of School Administrators (AASA) is the national association for superintendents and was founded in 1865. It is headquartered in the following location:

American Association of School Administrators
1615 Duke Street
Alexandria, VA 22314
1-703-875-0772

Many superintendents belong to AASA and read its monthly publication *School Administrator: Essential Insights and Commentary for School System Leaders.*

Nearly two decades ago, Lunenburg and Ornstein wrote of the "increased lobbying efforts" of NASB and AASA in the political process, especially at the gubernatorial candidate level (1996, p. 260). The reality of the need for involvement in state and national politics is greater today for board members and superintendents as state and national issues greatly affect local decision making.

EXTERNAL EXPERTS

Two nationally known external experts or consultants, Doug Eadie and Don McAdams, are widely published and considered experts in the area of board/superintendent interactions. Eadie (2007) has written several books and articles on school district governance, including *Meeting the Governing Challenge: Applying the High Impact Governing Model in Your Organization*, which is a relevant work that is intended for not-for-profit boards and school boards. In this book, Eadie describes the role of the CEO and leadership team and states that a board-savvy CEO is the team captain. He places special emphasis on the CEO's attitude and the importance of planning. The purpose of the board is also clearly described.

Readers may be interested in checking the Doug Eadie and Company website (www.dougeadie.com), which describes executive leadership consulting and a strategic approach for change management. Included on the website are areas of emphasis such as high-impact governing and involving your board in leading change. Eadie is a regular contributor to the *American School Board Journal*. An example of an article is "Special Requests," in the *American School Board Journal* (2012).

Donald R. McAdams is chairman and founder of the Center for Reform of School Systems (www.crss.org). His Houston-based organization is "dedicated to preparing school board members and superintendents to transform their districts into high-performing organizations that produce high student achievement" (www.crss.org).

McAdams has served as a school board member and is a university professor and author. He has also been appointed to several state and national commissions and task forces focusing on school improvement efforts. McAdams is considered a national expert on school board governance and is a regular contributor to the *School Administrator*. An example of an article is: "When Is It Time to Say Goodbye?" (2012).

There are numerous educational experts at the local, state, and national levels. External experts are a potentially excellent resource for board members and superintendents. Individuals seeking the assistance of external experts are encouraged to talk about such resources with colleagues, consult websites, and speak with state executive directors.

OTHER RESOURCES

There are numerous examples of well-developed and researched resources that support board and superintendent interactions. One example that has received considerable attention was developed by John Carver, founder of the Carver Policy Governance Model (www.carvergovernance.com). The Carver Model has received extensive use and acclaim in the areas of business, higher education, and other arenas.

The Carver website indicates the model is "an integrated board leadership paradigm," which is a "groundbreaking model of governance designed to empower boards of directors to fulfill their obligation of accountability for the organization they govern" (www.carvergovernance.com). CEO evaluation is addressed as well as board meetings and the relationship of the board to the CEO. Carver has an extensive list of resources for "inequity corporations" and nonprofit governmental organizations. Materials include books, articles, training session information, and more.

SEARCH FIRMS

Hiring a superintendent is a primary function of the school board. A school board may choose to conduct the search on its own or may hire a search firm to coordinate the selection process when hiring a new superintendent. Board members considering a superintendent selection, as well as a current or aspiring superintendent seeking a position, may find a search firm to be a valuable resource.

For example, we presented the overview from one state, Colorado, describing how state organizations can serve as resources. We examined the website of Colorado's two state-level associations, which include hiring and search firm information. The Colorado CASE/CASSA lists openings for a wide range of education positions. The Colorado CASB describes detailed services available to boards seeking a new superintendent. A job search process listing eight discrete steps is provided. There is also a reference list for those districts seeking an interim superintendent.

The state associations for school boards and the state associations for superintendents are excellent resources when seeking a search firm. In addition, certain trade journals include listings of superintendent positions available and firms conducting the searches.

Thomas E. Glass of Memphis University (2012) conducted a scholarly study of issues relating to superintendent and school board leadership. Included in his study is an important analysis of superintendent turnover, the applicant pool, the search process, the "new" superintendent, board presidents, and boards. Glass also includes seven critical policy considerations regarding the superintendent selection process that can be useful as boards consider the type of hiring procedures and resources they will use.

Glass's (2012) policy considerations focus on studying the reasons for high superintendent turnover or "churning" in some districts, and the time demands of board service, especially for the board president. Glass also lists the need for more training for boards in the hiring process, and the possibility of forwarding district superintendent search information to the state education department for review and study to improve the hiring process. Glass's work is an example of the type of academic research that may be helpful to boards and superintendents.

HIGHER EDUCATION INSTITUTIONS

It is very important to recognize the important role colleges and universities may have in providing school boards and superintendents with the opportunity to enhance the board/superintendent interaction. It goes without saying that university faculty play a critical role in studying the academic factors that may contribute to effective school improvement. Countless articles and books are published each year in the world of academia and many have application to the real world of PK–12 public education.

IN THE NEWS

Public school issues receive extensive traditional media and social media coverage on a daily basis. Board members and superintendents are encouraged to set aside time to read and listen to media reports. National politicians, governors, teacher union leaders, professors, and local citizens are continually expressing their opinions about public schools. We hope board members and superintendents enjoy the conversation!

SUMMARY

Each state has a school board and superintendent association. There are two national associations, which continue to be vibrant: NSBA and AASA. Board members and superintendents are strongly encouraged to have a familiarity with and working knowledge of state and national associations.

It is also highly likely that at some time board members and superintendents will want to and need to consider enlisting the services of external experts, search firms, and higher education institutions. We have provided a brief overview of resources we believe can be useful in the process of seeking valuable, pertinent information regarding board/superintendent interactions.

REFERENCES

Eadie, D. (2007). *Meeting the governing challenge: Applying the high impact governing model in your organization.* Oldham, FL: Governance Edge Publication.

Eadie, D. (2012). Special requests. *American School Board Journal* 199(12), 27–28.

Glass, T. E. (2012) *School board presidents and their view of the superintendency.* Washington, DC: Education Commission of the States.

Lunenburg, F. C., and Orstein, A. C. (1996). *Educational administration concepts and practices* (2nd ed.). Belmont, CA: Wadsworth Publishing.

McAdams, D. (2012) When is it time to say good-bye? *School Administrator* 36(11), 12.

10

RESOURCES, BOOKS, ARTICLES, DISSERTATIONS, AND SUMMARY OF SELECTED RESEARCH

There are many informative and helpful resources for school board members and superintendents to study and utilize. This chapter lists the references used or considered for use in this book and provides an extensive, but not exhaustive, list of the many resources available to board members and superintendents.

BOOKS

Adelman, H. S., and Taylor, L. (2004a). *District superintendents and the school improvement problem of addressing barriers to learning.* Los Angeles: Center for Mental Health in Schools at UCLA. http://smhp.psych.ucla.edu.

Adelman, H., and Taylor, L. (2004b). *Enhancing a school board's focus on addressing barriers to learning and teaching.* Los Angeles: Center of Mental Health in Schools at UCLA.

Adelman, H. S., and Taylor, L. (2004c). *Restructuring boards of education to enhance schools' effectiveness in addressing barriers to student learning.* Los Angeles: Center for Mental Health in Schools at UCLA. http://smhp.psych.ucla.edu.

Adelman, H. S., and Taylor, L. (2006a). *The implementation guide to student learning supports in the classroom and school wide*. Thousand Oaks, CA: Corwin Press.

Adelman, H. S., and Taylor, L. (2006b). *The school leader's guide to student learning supports*. Thousand Oaks, CA: Corwin Press.

Adelman, H. S., and Taylor, L. (2008). *Rebuilding for learning: Addressing barriers to learning and teaching and re-engaging students*. New York: Scholastic.

Adelman, H., and Taylor, L. (2011). *District superintendents and the school improvement problem of addressing barriers to learning*. Los Angeles: Center of Mental Health in Schools at UCLA.

Brandt, R. M. (1990). *A close up look: Third party evaluation of program components*. Retrieved from ERIC Database (ED324288).

Brown, M., and Heywood, J. S. (2002). Paying for performance: Setting the stage. In M. Brown and J. S. Heywood (Eds.), *Paying for performance: An international comparison* (pp. 3–15). Armonk, NY: M. E. Sharpe.

Cambron-McCabe, Cunningham, L. L., Harvey, J., and Koff, R. H. (2005). *The Superintendent's Field Book*. Thousand Oaks, CA: Corwin Press.

Clay, M. V., and Soldwedel, P. (2008). *How to encourage school board accountability*. Bloomington, IN: Solution Tree Press.

Conley, S., and Odden, A. (1994). *Linking teacher compensation to teacher career development*. Retrieved from ERIC Database (ED380895).

Darling-Hammond, L. (2006a). *Powerful teacher education: Lessons from exemplary programs*. San Francisco: Jossey-Bass.

DuFour, R., DuFour, R., and Eaker, R. (2008). *Revisiting professional learning communities at work*. Bloomington, IN: Solution Tree.

Eadie, D. (2001). *Extraordinary board leadership: The seven keys to high impact governance*. Gaithersburg, MD: Aspen.

Eadie, D. (2004). *High-impact governing in a nutshell: 17 questions that board members and CEOs frequently ask*. Washington, DC: American Society of Association Executives.

Eadie, D. (2007). *Meeting the governing challenge: Applying the high impact governing model to your organization*. Oldham, FL: Governance Edge Publications.

ECS. (1998). *Stages of implementation of standards led education.* Denver, CO: Education Commission of the States.

Epstein, N. (2004). *Who's in charge?: The tangled web of school governance and policy.* Washington, DC: Brookings Institution Press.

Evert, T. F., and Van Deuren, A. E. (2012). *Making external experts work: Solutions for district leaders.* Lanham, MD: Rowman & Littlefield.

French, R. L. (1985). Career ladder plans. In P. R. Burden (Ed.), *Establishing career ladders in teaching* (pp. 18–33). Springfield, IL: Charles C. Scott.

Gladwell, M. (2013). *David and Goliath.* New York: Little, Brown.

Glass, T. E. (2012). *School board presidents and their view of the superintendency.* Washington, DC: Education Commission of the States.

Glazerman, S., and Seifullah, A. (2012). *An evaluation of the Chicago teacher advancement program (Chicago TAP) after four years.* Final report. Mathematica Policy Research, Inc. Retrieved from ERIC Database (ED530098).

Golarz, R., and Golarz, M. (1995). *The power of participation: Improving schools in a democratic society.* Champaign, IL: Research Press.

Golarz, R., and Golarz, M. (2011). *Sweet land of liberty.* Bloomington, IN: AuthorHouse Publishing Co.

Golarz, R., and Golarz, M. (2012). *The problem isn't teachers.* Bloomington, IN: AuthorHouse Publishing Co.

Gratz, D. B. (2009a). *The perils and promise of performance pay: Making education compensation work.* Lanham, MD: Rowman & Littlefield Education.

Hassel, B. C. (2002). *Better pay for better teaching: Making teaching compensation pay off in the age of accountability.* Washington, DC: Progressive Policy Institute 21st Century Schools Project.

Hirsch, E. (2006). *Recruiting and retaining teachers in Alabama: Educators on what it will take to staff all classrooms with quality teachers.* Chapel Hill, NC: Southeast Center for Teaching Quality.

Hoyle, J. R., Bjork, L. G., Collier, V., and Glass, T. (2005). *The superintendent as CEO: Standards-based performance.* Thousand Oaks, CA: Corwin, American Association of School Administrator.

Inman, D. (1985). The rhetoric and reality of merit pay: Why are they different? In H. C. Johnson (Ed.), *Merit, money and teachers' careers* (pp. 41–56). Lanham, MD: University Press of America, Inc.

Johnson, S. M., and Papay, J. P. (2009). *Redesigning teacher pay: A system for the next generation of educators.* Washington, DC: Economic Policy Institute.

Kersten, T. A. (2010). *Stepping into administration: How to succeed in making the move.* Lanham, MD: Rowman & Littlefield.

Lunenburg, F. C., and Orstein, A. C. (1996). *Educational administration concepts and practices* (2nd ed.). Belmont, CA: Wadsworth Publishing.

Lunenburg, F. C., and Ornstein, A. C. (2012). *Educational administration concepts and practices.* Belmont, CA: Wadsworth Publishing.

Martin, I. (1996). *From couch to corporation: Becoming a successful corporate therapist.* New York, NY: Wiley & Sons, Inc.

Marzano, R. J. (2009). *Formative assessment and standards-based grading: Classroom strategies that work.* Bloomington, IN: Solution Tree.

Marzano, R. J., and Waters, T. (2009). *District leadership that works: Striking the right balance.* Bloomington, IN: Solution Tree Press.

Mayer, R. (2011). *How not to be a terrible school board member: Lessons for school administrators and board members.* Thousand Oaks, CA: Corwin Press (SAGE).

McAdams, R. P. (2010). *Exploring the myths and realities of today's schools.* Lanham, MD: Rowman & Littlefield.

McTighe, J., and Wiggins, G. (1999). *The understanding by design handbook.* Alexandria, VA: Association for Supervision & Curriculum Development.

Merriam-Webster's Dictionary.

Munson, L., Wells, C., Stern, R., and Griffith, L. (2012). *Common core curriculum maps in English language arts.* San Francisco: Jossey-Bass.

Murray, J. E., and Brown, K. (2003). *Paying teachers for their worth: Policies on teacher compensation at the school district and regional levels.* Retrieved from ERIC Database (ED482348).

The National Commission on Excellence in Education. (1983). *A nation at risk: The imperative for educational reform.* Washington, DC: U.S. Department of Education.

National School Boards Association. (2006). *Becoming a better board member: A guide to effective school board service* (3rd ed.). Alexandria, VA: National School Boards Association.

Odden, A., and Kelley, C. (1997). *Paying teachers for what they know and do: New and smarter compensation strategies to improve schools.* Thousand Oaks, CA: Corwin Press.

Odden, A., and Kelley, C. (2002). *Paying teachers for what they know and do: New and smarter compensation strategies to improve schools* (2nd ed.). Thousand Oaks, CA: Corwin Press.

Popham, W. J. (2003). *Assessment for educational leaders.* Boston, MA: Pearson.

Prince, C. D. (2003). *Higher pay in hard-to-staff schools.* Lanham, MD: University Press of American, Inc.

Reeves, D. (2010a). *Elements of grading: A guide to effective practice.* Bloomington, IN: Solution Tree Press.

Reeves, D. (2010b). *Transforming professional development into student results.* Alexandria, VA: Association for Supervision & Curriculum Development.

Reeves, R. (2006). *What every rookie superintendent should know.* Lanham, MD: Rowman & Littlefield.

Senge, P. (1994). *The fifth discipline.* New York, NY: Doubleday.

Smith, S., Chavez, A., and Seaman, G. (2012). *Teacher as architect.* Chicago, IL: Modern Teacher Press.

Sojourner, A., West, K., and Mykerezi, E. (2011). *When does teacher incentive pay raise student achievement? Evidence from Minnesota's Q-comp program.* Retrieved from ERIC Database (ED528841).

Solmon, L. C., and Podgursky, M. (2000). *The pros and cons of performance-based compensation.* Retrieved from ERIC Database (ED445393).

Sperry, L. (1996). *Corporate therapy and consulting.* New York, NY: Brunner/Mazel, Inc.

Springer, M. G. (2009). *Performance incentives: Their growing impact on American K–12 education.* Washington, DC: Brookings Institution Press.

Springer, M. G., Ballou, D., Hamilton, L., Le, V., Lockwood, J. R., McCaffrey, D., Pepper, M., and Stecher, B. (2010). *Teacher pay for performance: Experimental evidence from the project on incentives in teaching.* Nashville, TN: National Center on Performance Incentives at Vanderbilt University.

Stronge, J. H., Gareis, C., and Little, C. (2006). *Teacher pay and teacher quality: Attracting, developing, and retaining the best teachers.* Thousand Oaks, CA: Corwin Press.

Taylor, L., Springer, M., and Ehlert, M. (2009). Teacher-designed performance-pay in Texas. In M. G. Springer (Ed.), *Performance incentives: Their growing impact on American K–12 education* (pp. 191–223). Washington, DC: Brookings Institution Press.

Townsend, R. S., Johnston, G. L., Gross, G. E., Lynch, P., Garcy, L., Roberts, B., and Novotney, P. B. (2006). *Effective superintendent–school board practices: Strategies for developing and maintaining good relationships with your board.* Thousand Oaks, CA: Corwin Press (SAGE).

Wiggins, G. (2005). *The understanding by design guide to creating high-quality units.* Alexandria, VA: Association for Supervision & Curriculum Development.

Wiggins, G., and McTighe, J. (2012). *The understanding by design guide to advanced concepts in creating and reviewing units (professional development).* Alexandria, VA: Association for Supervision & Curriculum Development.

ARTICLES

Argyris, C. (1991). Teaching smart people how to learn. *Harvard Business Review* 69(3), 99–109.

Ballou, D. (2001). Pay for performance in public and private schools. *Economics of Education Review* 20(1), 51–61.

Cohen, D. K., and Murnane, R. J. (1985). The merits of merit pay. *Public Interest* 80(3), 3–31.

Darling-Hammond, L. (1998). Teachers and teaching: Testing policy hypotheses from a national commission report. *Educational Researcher* 27(1), 5–15.

Darling-Hammond, L. (2006). Securing the right to learn: Policy and practice for powerful teaching and learning. *Educational Researcher* 35(7), 13–24.

Darling-Hammond, L., and Youngs, P. (2002). Defining "highly qualified teachers." What does "scientifically-based research" actually tell us? *Educational Researcher* 31(9), 13–25.

Dickson, L. (1990). *Student achievement and career ladder status.* Retrieved from ERIC Database (ED324775).

D'Orio, W. (2002). Holding school boards more accountable. *District Administration, Association of Educational Administrators.* Norwalk, CT.

Feldman, S. (2000). True merit pay. *National Journal 32*(11), 757.

Firestone, W. A. (1991, October). Merit pay and job enlargement as reforms: Incentives, implementation, and teacher response. *Educational Evaluation and Policy Analysis 13*(3), 269–88.

Firestone, W. A. (1994). Redesigning teacher salary systems for educational reform. *American Educational Research Journal 31*(3), 549–74.

Gratz, D. B. (2005). Lessons from Denver: The pay for performance pilot. *Phi Delta Kappan 86*(8), 569–81.

Gratz, D. B. (2009b, November). The problem with performance pay. *Educational Leadership 67*(3), 76–79.

Guthrie, J. W., and Springer, M. G. (2004). *A Nation at Risk* revisited: Did "wrong" reasoning result in "right" results? At what cost? *Peabody Journal of Education 79*(1), 7–35.

Iowa Association of School Boards [IASB] (2000). IASB's Lighthouse Study: School boards and student achievement. *Iowa School Board Compass 5*(2), 1–12.

Kelley, C., Heneman III, H., and Milanowski, A. (2002). Teacher motivation and school-based performance awards. *Education Administration Quarterly 38*(3), 372–401.

Kelley, C., and Odden, A. (1995). *Reinventing teacher compensation systems. CPRE Finance Briefs.* Retrieved from ERIC Database (ED387910).

Kohn, A. (2003, September 17). The folly of merit pay. *Education Week.* Retrieved from http://www.edweek.org.

Land, D. (2002, January). Local school boards under review: Their role and effectiveness in relation to students' academic achievement. Johns Hopkins University, Report No. 56.

Mayer, R. (2013). A board member overdoes his homework. *School Administrator 12.*

McAdams, D. R. (2008). Getting your board out of micromanagement. *The School Administrator 65*(10).

McAdams, D., (2012). When is it time to say goodbye? *School Administrator 36*(11), 12.

McCollum, S. (2001, February). How merit pay improves education. *Educational Leadership* 58(5), 21–24.

Mellon, E. (2010, January 27). HISD to pay out more than $40 million in bonuses. *Houston Chronicle*. Retrieved from http://www.chron.com.

Milanowski, A. (2002). *The varieties of knowledge and skill-based pay design: A comparison of seven new pay systems for K–12 teachers.* Retrieved from ERIC Database (ED477655).

Milken, L. (2000). *Teaching as the opportunity: The teacher advancement program.* Retrieved from ERIC Database (ED456116).

Moscinski, D. (2013, June). Is school board unity possible? *American School Board Journal*, Archive.

Murnane, R. J., and Cohen, D. K. (1986). Merit pay and the evaluation problem: Why most merit pay plans fail and few survive. *Harvard Educational Review* 56(1), 1–17.

Odden, A. (2000). New and better forms of teacher compensation are possible. *Phi Delta Kappan* 81(5), 361–66.

Odden, A., and Wallace, M. (2004). Experimenting with teacher compensation. *School Administrator* 61(9), 24–28.

Podgursky, M. J., and Springer, M. G., (2006). Teacher performance pay: A review. Working Paper 2006-01. Nashville, TN: National Center on Performance Incentives at Vanderbilt University.

Popham, W. J. (2009). Assessment literacy for teachers: Faddish or fundamental? *Theory into Practice* 48(1), 4–11.

Pringle, H. R. (2013). Five ways to unknowingly undermine your board. *School Administrator* 70(4), 10.

Protsik, J. (1995). History of teacher pay and incentive reforms. Madison, WI: *Consortium for Policy Research in Education*. Retrieved from ERIC Database (ED380894).

Ramirez, A. (2010/2011, December/January). Merit pay misfires. *Educational Leadership* 68(4), 55–58.

Ritsche, D. (2001). Wisconsin Briefs from the Legislative Reference Bureau. LRB-01-WB-4, January 2001.

Rothstein, D., and Santana, L. (2011). Teaching students to ask their own questions. *Harvard Education Letter* 27(5).

This item came off the Internet at this location: http://hepg.org/hel-home/issues/27_5/helarticle/teaching-students-to-ask-their-own-questions_507#home.

Sheehan, B. A. (2013). Why do superintendents leave? *The American School Board Journal.* Retrieved from http://mydigimag.rrd.com/display_article.php?id=1310669.

Sherman, R., Wells, L. R., and Dedrick, C. S., (2012). Succession planning done right. *American School Board Journal* 199(6), 26–27.

Taylor, L., Springer, M., and Ehlert, M. (2008). Characteristics and determinants of teacher-designed pay for performance plans: Evidence from Texas' Governor's Educator Excellence Grant (GEEG) program. Working Paper 2008-26. Nashville, TN: National Center on Performance Incentives at Vanderbilt University.

Wilms, W. W., and Chapleau, R. R. (1999, November). The illusion of paying teachers for student performance. *Education Week* 19(10), 34, 48.

Yuan, K., Le, V., McCaffrey, D. F., Marsh, J. A., Hamilton, L. S., Stecher, B. M., and Springer, M. G. (2013). Incentive pay programs do not affect teacher motivation or reported practices: Results from three randomized studies. *Educational Evaluation and Policy Analysis* 35(1), 3.

DISSERTATIONS

For this book, the following dissertations served as the basis for chapters or as references.

Chang, R. G. L. (1999). *Current teachers' compensation systems and their perceived effects on motivation.* PhD dissertation, University of Southern California. Available from ProQuest Dissertations and Theses database (UMI No. 3110946).

Dalal, A. D. (2008). *School implementation of a board-adopted inquiry process to improve student learning.* Unpublished EdD, University of California, San Diego, San Diego State University and California State University, San Marcos.

Olson, Dan (2014). *Examination of Wisconsin school district superintendent perceptions regarding alternative teacher compensation systems.* Doctoral dissertation, Edgewood College, Madison, Wisconsin.

Wellnitz, D. (2008). *Resource mapping and management to address barriers to learning: An intervention for systemic change.* EdD dissertation, Edgewood College, Madison, Wisconsin.

WEBSITES

Center for Educator Compensation Reform. (2012). Retrieved from http://www.cecr.ed.gov.
Consortium for Policy Research in Education. (2012). Retrieved from http://www.cpre.org.
Dewitt, P. (July 22, 2013). Schools need to be more consultant savvy. *Education Week Blogs.* Retrieved from http://www.edweek.org/ew/section/blogs/index.html.
Harris, D.C. (2007). *The promises and pitfalls of alternative teacher compensation approaches.* East Lansing, MI: The Great Lakes Center for Education Research & Practice. Retrieved from http://www.greatlakescenter.org.
Herman-Lockwood, M. (2014, March). Enforcing board member responsibilities, published by the Nonprofit Risk Management Center, www.nonprofitrisk.org.
No Child Left Behind (NCLB) Act of 2001, Pub. L. No. 107-110, §115, Stat. 1425 (2002). Retrieved from http://www2.ed.gov/legislation/esea02/107-110.pdf.
ProComp. (2012). Retrieved from http://denverprocomp.dpsk12.org.
U.S. Department of Education. (2012). *Federal student aid: Teacher loan forgiveness.* Retrieved from http://studentaid.ed.gov/repay-loans/forgiveness-cancellation/charts/teacher.
Wisconsin Center for Education Research. (2008). *Approaches to alternative teachers compensation: Promises and pitfalls.* Retrieved from http://www.wcer.wisc.edu.

SUMMARY OF SELECTED RESEARCH 2000–2010

There are many excellent resources available that focus primarily on either effective board service or the superintendency. The following review includes both perspectives. It is not meant to be exhaustive; rather, it provides an overview of research reported during the period from 2000 to 2010.

Doug Eadie

Doug Eadie is a well-known scholar of board/superintendent relations. In his work *Eight Keys to an Extraordinary Board-Superintendent Partnership* (2003), Eadie writes to a superintendent audience about the following eight keys to creating a good working relationship with the board: (1) put partnership at the top of your list, (2) specialize in governing business, (3) empower your board, (4) turn board members into owners, (5) spice up the governing stew, (6) get your senior administration on board, (7) keep expectations in sync, and (8) stay on the high-growth plan.

In his work *Extraordinary Board Leadership: The Keys to High-Impact Governance* (2008), he focuses on the teamwork necessary to create a high-impact board that positively affects student achievement. Eadie stresses the need for clarity in board work and encourages boards to learn the art of governance as well as the importance of building and maintaining a healthy board/CEO partnership. Most important, Eadie contends that boards must develop their "performance management capacity."

Throughout his work, Eadie stresses the importance of partnerships, the role of the board president, and being adaptable to the inevitable changes that will take place on the board over time. Superintendents need to be adaptable and flexible to different board member agendas and leadership styles, and to do their best to empower the board by giving them a sense of real ownership at a time when boards are arguably more disempowered than ever before in a climate of increasing federal and state mandates.

Critical to the board/superintendent relationship and high-impact governing is the need for superintendents to recognize the realities boards face. Eadie (2004) indicates that leaders should expect board resistance because boards tend to have strong affiliations and a sense of ownership of particular programs and/or are satisfied with the status quo. Getting boards moving from "stuck" or ineffective to high impact often requires superintendent encouragement of board development. Board development includes looking at long-range planning; the "as is" of the current school district and the "to be" of the future for the school district. It also involves getting boards involved in the here and now by assessing how well the district is doing in terms of programs, finance, and administration.

Eadie (2004) also recognizes the importance of emotional bonding, stating that "strangers don't make good team members" (p. 43). Open meeting laws make relationship building among board members particularly challenging, especially when most of their interactions as a board are held in an open forum. He suggests that building information interactions with board meetings, sharing biographies, holding retreats, and using standing committees can help board members bond by spending time together and interacting in smaller groups.

Finally, Eadie acknowledges the importance of attracting individuals to board service who will serve the community and board well, and the importance of selecting a leader who is a good fit for the board and the district. He believes that the board/superintendent partnership is fragile because (1) members of the leadership team tend to have strong personalities and egos, and (2) the issues at hand are high stakes and complex.

Noel Epstein

Noel Epstein's (2007) book titled *Who's in Charge Here?* contains nine chapters, provides a big-picture discussion and analysis of board/superintendent issues, and covers issues including governance, policymaking, and student achievement past and present.

The book includes a detailed history of governance in American education (Kirst, chapter 2). The important fundamental question of who should be in charge of schools is presented as well as several other complex topics confounding the issue of governance, including distrust, politics, equity, teacher organizations, student achievement, increased state involvement, and increased federalization of education.

Hill (chapter 4) analyzes the roles of families, schools, districts, and state/federal government in board governance, and strengths and weaknesses of each entity as related to board service. Using each entity as a framework, Hill describes what each does well in relation to the health of school districts and board service, and what each does poorly. For example, families support students emotionally and demand schooling that is appropriate for each child's needs; however, families do not create well-ordered curricula and do not apply professional expertise to the process of teaching. This chapter highlights one of the many layers of complexity that boards and superintendents must address on a daily basis.

Cuban (chapter 5) discusses student achievement in the context of centralized policymaking that has become the ever-increasing norm for establishing standards for student achievement and classroom gains. Cuban addresses three underlying assumptions that policymakers make about American education: (1) American students have mediocre performance, which places U.S. economic performance in jeopardy; (2) the United States has relaxed academic standards, has a negative attitude toward competition, and has been unaccountable for student outcomes and lacks the ability and will to grasp the situation in order to solve these issues; and (3) more authority should be shifted to state and federal agencies to establish standards, increase testing, and hold schools accountable while promoting more competition among schools.

In subsequent years, our country has seen these assumptions play out and they have created more complexity for boards and superintendents as increased accountability and testing, school choice, and Common Core State Standards become a reality and are being implemented. However, Cuban makes excellent arguments as to why these assumptions are largely mistaken, and while they underpin much of today's educational realities, boards and superintendents will do well to question the implementation of each.

Rene Townsend, Gloria Johnston, Gwen Gross, Peggy Lynch, Lorraine Garcy, Benita Roberts, and Patricia Novotney

Townsend and colleagues (2006) wrote *Effective Superintendent-School Board Practices*, a book that explains the nuts and bolts of board/superintendent interactions. This work focuses on relationship building, creating a team, maintaining focus, managing conflicts, and succession planning. The authors suggest that relationship building is a continuous process, and that superintendents spent 20 to 25 percent of their time working directly with the board. They discuss the challenges new board members face and the role of the superintendent in reducing conflict among board members.

Townsend and colleagues discuss the complexity of the board/superintendent partnership in very practical terms, and discuss how to interact without surprises, how to stay focused on a strategic plan, consensus building, the importance of board self-evaluation, role clarity, gossip, and "rebel board members." This book includes vignettes, analysis, action steps, key strategies, and an evaluation guide for both boards and superintendents. This work contains examples and discussion questions, and captures the realities of board/superintendent interactions in the twenty-first century.

Thomas Alsbury

Alsbury's (2008) highly academic work, *The Future of School Board Governance: Relevancy and Revelation*, systematically details the complexities of the board/superintendent partnership in the area of governance. Nineteen contributors, largely from the world of school administration or higher education, focus on student achievement and school boards. An emphasis on school board politics is evident throughout the work.

Delegardelle (chapter 10) details the groundbreaking work of the Lighthouse Project in Iowa, where key linkages between boards and student learning were established indicating that school boards do indeed have an effect on student achievement. The Lighthouse Inquiry identified five main functions of school boards: (1) boards set clear expectations; (2) boards hold systems accountable; (3) boards create conditions for success; (4) boards build the collective will to succeed; and (5) boards learn as a team.

Stringfield (chapter 13) acknowledges that much of the role of a board member involves tedious homework, and that the three main leverages board members have are the superintendent contract, the budget, and civic engagement. This book takes the reader through the history of board service, and ultimately articulates the need for more research on culture clashes, local history, and the uniqueness of each school district (Peterson and Fusarelli, chapter 5).

Nancy Walser

The Essential School Board Book (2009) describes sixteen school districts with high-functioning boards across the United States. Both large and small school districts are represented, including Boston, Massachusetts; Atlanta, Georgia; Elk Mound, Wisconsin; LaCrosse, Wisconsin; and Gallatin County, Kentucky. The preface is written by William J. Phalen, Sr. of the Calvert County, Maryland, Board of Education, and includes a "top ten list" that has a humorous edge, but can also be serious food for thought:

Top Ten Reasons to Be a Board Member

10. Because I really like to sit on hard chairs for extended periods of time.
9. Because there are very few foods that I don't enjoy, or at least won't eat.
8. Because I enjoy being at numerous evening events (you may have a problem if your spouse enjoys you being at these events).
7. Because I like a challenge.
6. Because educators made a real difference in my life
5. Because I have the gift to listen, hear, and understand positions that are different from my own.
4. Because I have the ability to be ardent in my beliefs or opinions, but also the ability to compromise when necessary.
3. Because I want our children and young people to be successful in school and I don't care who gets the credit.
2. Because I realize that every child has the ability and right to as good an education as we can provide.
1. Because I believe I can make a difference in the education of the children and young people where I live.

This work discusses board practices that make a difference, including seven conditions for school renewal central to student achievement. The focus is on board collaboration, staying focused on achievement, setting and meeting goals, and using data throughout the process. Ethics, norms, values, self-policing, and problem solving are also addressed under the context of avoiding pitfalls that make boards unproductive.

Finally, Walser discusses the importance of cultivating citizens for board service and attracting educationally minded individuals to board service. This section addresses veteran board members who seek to encourage other individuals to run for office, and the importance of belief in student achievement, and understanding of the value of education, critical thinking and analytical ability, and the need to be a team player willing to leave the ego at the door.

Richard E. Mayer

Mayer (2008) offers insights into board/superintendents based on his twenty-eight years of service as a board member in a California K–12 district with 3,500 students. *How Not to Be a Terrible School Board Member: Lessons for School Administrators and Board Members* takes a humorous and practical look at board service from the perspective of what *not* to do. Twenty-eight terrible habits are divided into the following four sections: (1) terrible district teamwork, (2) terrible board teamwork, (3) terrible PR, and (4) terrible personal style. These terrible habits include: (1) humiliate a district employee in public, (2) disrespect a fellow board member, (3) represent your support group, and (4) ignore minor conflicts of interest. These items are laced with humor but can deliver a powerful collection of flashbacks for veteran board members and superintendents.

Mayer includes important reasons to run for board service and articulates good habits of board service as well. He provides eleven pledges that board members should make, including reading lots of materials, attending special events, making informed decisions, and playing by the rules. The lessons are practical, clear, and help to establish a good foundation for board service.

Richard McAdams

McAdams (2010) addresses school board effectiveness in *Exploring the Myths and Realities of Today's Schools: A Candid Review of the Challenges Educators Face*. An excellent historical view of the evolution of education in America is provided. He pays particular attention to school board development, stating that a critical board duty is to "first and, most important, attract and employ an excellent superintendent" (p. 97). The impact of a poor performing board is described. The positive benefits and far-reaching influence of a strong board with integrity and competence is also described.

McAdams contends that 50 percent of boards are in the mid-range of effectiveness, 25 percent are dysfunctional, and 25 percent perform quite well. While it takes time for a board to function smoothly, "a dysfunctional board can negatively affect the educational program in less than a year" (p. 98). He acknowledges that it can take a long time for a community to recover from the effects of a poor school board. He concludes chapter 11 by stating that "school boards cannot control schools in the technical sense of the term, but they do influence school district operations in ways that can materially affect school district quality" (p. 98).

McAdams includes interesting historical and statistical information in this work. For example, more than 100,000 citizens serve nationally as board members at any given time and two out of three serve without compensation. Board members serve an average of seven years, 60 percent are men, and board members are typically better educated than their publics. Citizens directly elect 94 percent of boards. The average board member works on board activities about twenty-five hours per month. Partisan politics are found in urban districts but are far less common in rural and suburban areas.

An important aspect of this book is the concept of the "virtual indifference" (p. 102) the public has toward schools. The role of board members as community leaders is important as board members serve as ambassadors for the schools in the eyes of the community.

The importance of the board's role in influencing curriculum is also discussed. There are three ways that boards can influence curriculum: (1) with oversight; (2) with encouragement and regular achievement reports; and (3) for the board to establish benchmarks for student achievement in the area of curriculum. In addition, McAdams stresses that the board has significant financial responsibility and that there are relatively few discretionary dollars left after staffing costs are calculated.

McAdams discusses the importance of the trustee role board members play and encourages board members to have parents and citizens follow the established chain of command when expressing grievances. He discusses how one or two negative board members can upset the balance of the board/superintendent relationship and undermine "the respect and confidence that a community would like to have in its public officials" (p. 106).

Finally, McAdams describes a high-functioning board and provides a comprehensive description of the role of the superintendent. He addresses the issue of a high-functioning board appearing to "rubber stamp" (p. 108) every superintendent request. Ultimately, McAdams acknowledges that the most critical factor to the success of a superintendent is his or her relationship with the board. When a superintendent makes a mistake, he or she must take blame and move forward. The effective superintendent is described in detail and McAdams places emphasis on the inspirational aspects of the position. Three guidelines for superintendents new to the position include being truthful, having a sense of humor, and always being ready and willing to lose the job if it is the cost of standing up for your principles.

ABOUT THE CONTRIBUTORS

EDITORS

Dr. **Amy E. Van Deuren** holds a doctorate in educational leadership from National Louis University and a master's degree in music education and law from the University of Utah. She has experience as a high school band director, lawyer, and business owner. She served as faculty member and administrator at National Louis University before taking a position as the principal at West Allis Central High School in the West Allis-West Milwaukee School District. Dr. Van Deuren has coauthored several books on music education and educational leadership, including *Music Education Dictionary*, *Wind Talk for Woodwinds*, *Wind Talk for Brass*, *Making External Experts Work*, and *Thriving as a Superintendent*.

Dr. **Thomas F. Evert** received his doctorate from the University of Wisconsin-Madison in educational psychology. He served as a school psychologist, high school principal, director of student services, and superintendent in three districts in Wisconsin, and retired after serving fourteen years as a superintendent. Dr. Evert currently serves as an instructor, dissertation advisor, and dissertation liaison at Edgewood

College. He coauthored two books on educational leadership, *Making External Experts Work* and *Thriving as a Superintendent*.

Dr. **Bette A. Lang** holds her doctorate in educational administration from Marquette University and her master's and specialists' degrees from the University of Wisconsin–Superior. She has experience as a teacher, assistant principal, middle and high school principal, director of instruction, and superintendent in six school districts in Wisconsin. She retired after serving sixteen years as a superintendent in four districts. Dr. Lang is currently an instructor, dissertation advisor, and dissertation liaison at Edgewood College.

CONTRIBUTORS

Dr. **Raymond Golarz** holds a bachelor's degree in both sociology and education from St. Joseph's College in Indiana. He received a master's degree and a doctorate in education from Indiana University. Dr. Golarz has teaching experience at the elementary, middle school, high school, and university levels. Dr. Golarz has been an administrator in three Indiana school systems. In 1984, he was appointed assistant superintendent in Hammond. From 1986 to 1989 he served as superintendent in Hobart. In 1989 he accepted a position as superintendent of Richmond Community Schools in Richmond, Indiana. In all three school systems he helped introduce and develop participatory governance. Dr. Golarz and his wife, Dr. Marion Golarz, have done extensive work with participatory governance and promoting teacher empowerment through his teaching, presentations, and workshops.

Dr. **Daniel W. Olson** holds his doctorate in educational leadership from Edgewood College. His doctoral research focused on alternative compensation models, culminating in his dissertation, titled *Examination of Wisconsin School District Superintendent Perceptions Regarding Alternative Teacher Compensation Systems*. Dr. Olson currently serves as the superintendent of the Monona Grove School District in Monona, Wisconsin. Prior experience includes serving as the superintendent of the Campbellsport School District and as high school principal in the Northern Ozaukee School District, both in Wisconsin. Professional interests include human resource development and equity in education. Personal interests and hobbies include golfing, skiing, biking, and attending sporting events.

Dr. **Linda Nortier** holds a doctorate in education from George Williams College of Aurora University. Her research analyzed the elements of professional development and positioning professional learning as the unifying process of a school district's organization. Dr. Nortier currently serves as the Education Outreach Coordinator for the University of Wisconsin–Whitewater, assisting school districts and university faculty in working together to improve teaching and learning. She has served in many K–12 positions from special education teacher to director of curriculum and instruction, and the director of instructional services at a regional education service agency in Wisconsin, CESA 2. In addition, Dr. Nortier has extensive experience teaching education courses at the undergraduate and graduate levels.

Dr. **Valerie Schmitz** earned her PhD from Capella University with a dissertation titled *Examination of Multiple Intelligences in the Cisco Network Academy* and her EdD from National Louis University with a dissertation titled *Emergence of Charter School Pedagogies in Wisconsin*. Her current position is Effectiveness Project Coordinator at CESA 6 in Oshkosh, Wisconsin. Dr. Schmitz is the co-founder of Teach Me Peace, Inc. and Learning Journeys, LLC. Her professional work includes that of middle school teacher, technology director, instructional designer, principal eLearning director, evaluator of educator effectiveness, school board member, and university instructor at Purdue University, Pepperdine University, and National Louis University. She has written and presented internationally on social networking organizational systems, technology integration, project based learning, and global education. She is also an alumnus of Authentic Leadership in Action and HumaNext, and she co-facilitates the United Nations University for Peace Centre's online course, *Social Media for Social Innovation and Face to Face Education 2.0*.

Dr. **Denise L. Wellnitz** holds her doctorate in educational leadership from Edgewood College. Her research focused on mapping and managing barriers to learning and interventions for systemic change. Her experience in education includes teaching and director of student services. Dr. Wellnitz is currently serving as superintendent for the Darlington, Wisconsin School District.

www.ingramcontent.com/pod-product-compliance
Lightning Source LLC
Chambersburg PA
CBHW030141240426
43672CB00005B/225